How's Your Family

Really Doing?

10 Keys
to a
Happy
Loving
Family

Don MacMannis, Ph.D.
Debra Manchester MacMannis, M.S.W.

Advance Praise for
How's Your Family Really Doing?

*Excellent, informative, helpful, and well written. As a psychologist who has seen many children and families in therapy, I was delighted to read **How's Your Family Really Doing?** It is a wonderful resource that reflects the insights of two skilled and experienced family clinicians.*

The book includes not only practical, realistic ideas for enriching one's family life, but also a 50-point self-assessment instrument to examine one's family's strengths and the areas that require improvement. It is written in a reader-friendly manner that will be read and re-read by families and professionals alike. Don and Debra are to be commended for their impressive book.

-Robert Brooks, Ph.D., Psychologist, Faculty of Harvard Medical School
Co-author of *Raising Resilient Children*, and Co-author of *The Power of Resilience*

*The 10 Keys provided in **How's Your Family Really Doing?** will ensure the answer is, "Getting better all the time." These keys, such as Seeing the Positive, Balancing Closeness and Difference, Making Decisions, and Parenting Together, contain subtle insights that will appeal to even the most thoughtful and conscientious parents. Every key is backed up by very specific, practical steps just about everyone can realistically take. A brief quiz at the outset also helps parents identify their priority areas, so if you don't want to read the entire book, you can focus on what is most important to you right now.*

Don and Debra have harnessed their extensive clinical experience, their parenting wisdom, and what is obviously a strong sense of family to create a resource that will be of lasting value to parents, prospective parents, grandparents, and clinicians. It is welcoming, warm, and wise.

-Maurice J. Elias, Ph.D.
Author, *Emotionally Intelligent Parenting*
Director of Clinical Training, Rutgers University

ISBN-13: 978-1484012789
ISBN-10: 148401278X

Distributed by Create Space

Cover Design by Jen Brookman
Edited by Sheryl Tritten

Printed in the United States of America

Table of Contents

Foreword by Ron Taffel.. i

Introduction... v

Current Family Assessment and Analysis xi

Chapter One   Key #1 Talking and Listening 1

Chapter Two   Key #2 Expressing Feelings......................... 13

Chapter Three   Key #3 Adapting to Change......................... 35

Chapter Four   Key #4 Sharing Time Together 50

Chapter Five   Key #5 Who's in Charge? 60

Chapter Six   Key #6 Balancing Closeness and Distance... 84

Chapter Seven   Key #7 Accepting Differences..................... 99

Chapter Eight   Key #8 Seeing the Positive 113

Chapter Nine   Key #9 Effective Problem-solving 125

Chapter Ten   Key #10 Parenting Together....................... 135

Chapter Eleven   Echoes of the Past 156

Chapter Twelve   Making Changes 165

The Seed 174

Self-Help Resources 175

Bibliography 188

Index... 195

Acknowledgments... 204

About the Authors 206

Other Great Materials 208

FOREWORD

by Ron Taffel

Families are a lot like the weather. Sometimes warm and sunny, just as quickly turning cold and stormy. As Mark Twain once said, "A great, great deal has been said about the weather, but very little has ever been done." So, too, everyone constantly talks about their most important relationships, delighting when they're good, complaining when they're bad. Everyone wants to be in a happy family, but how do we create one—really?

The reason I offered to write the foreword for *How's Your Family Really Doing?* is because we have reached a point in time when parents, child professionals, and educators deserve to learn what is truly known about the characteristics and skill sets that comprise a healthy family.

Looking at the family from a historical perspective it becomes clear why this confusion-ending resource is particularly timely and relevant. Since World War II, there have been at least five major trends in parenting, education, and psychology. After the war, psychoanalytic models, which focused on individual pathology and family enmeshment, reigned over mental health clinics as well as in the professional literature. Kids and parents needed to be pried away from each other—separation was considered the antidote to "living under each other's skin." This movement gave way to the "dysfunctional family," partially a product of post-sixties unraveling in tight-knit family, community, and religious institutions. The emphasis now was on "tough love." Limits and hierarchy were the answers for acting-out kids who had been catered to by the psychoanalytic perspective before. Soon parenting approaches again gave way, now to the "self-esteem revolution," a product of discovering how many kids had been crushed by serious, and until then, hidden family abuse. In the seventies, praise became the watchword; each child was celebrated for his or her uniqueness. The eighties birthed "family values," in part a response to the perceived coddling and child-centeredness of the self-esteem revolution just before. Family values called for a return to teaching children traditional virtues—truth, honesty, and loyalty, among others. Parents once again were implored to be firmly and authoritatively in charge.

Despite the invaluable contributions these perspectives made to the field, as well as to the culture at large, each was in part a reaction to the one preceding; and, more often than not, diametrically opposed. The pendulum swung back and forth, and the public, both parents and professionals alike, were increasingly enlightened, yet confused at the same time.

Fast forward to the present. The new millennium has seen an explosion in what I call "the medicalization of childhood." Parents and professionals are on the lookout for a myriad of new labels, psychological problems increasingly understood as genetic, biological, and individual. Almost every child has some diagnosable disorder often leading to the use of newly discovered medications. Parents and child professionals are on a search-and-identify mission to figure out what's wrong with children of all ages and then "fix" them' as quickly as possible.

None of this is problematic in and of itself. In fact, the advances made are staggering, with each trend offering a great deal that furthers both parenting and treatment. The problem is that while we have amassed a tremendous amount of knowledge, with information literally available at our fingertips, there is more confusion than ever before. Everywhere I lecture around the country, whether my audience is made up of parents, child educators, or mental health professionals, I encounter the same phenomenon. There are always those who argue for the rightness of one point of view or perspective. The rest—and these represent the vast majority—are overwhelmed by the astonishing glut of information. Let's face it, every morning when we open our computer home pages, we find the results of yet another, often contradictory study that instructs us on what foods we should eat or avoid, what discipline technique we should use or not, and what new medication has just been introduced or just taken off the market.

In spite of all this information, or perhaps because of it, few clinicians are ever taught the basics about what makes a family function well and how to help families reach the universally sought-after goal of being happy together.

This is not part of the curriculum in most graduate programs, nor is it taught in parenting classes or workshops for clinicians. We all wish to create healthy, loving families, but we lack guidelines in both our professional training and in the popular culture to identify essential threads. Because of this, when I first spoke with Debra and Don about *How's Your Family Really Doing?*, I was immediately drawn to their organizing concept. The book clearly answers many of the questions I continue to get from thousands of adults in my clinical practice as psychologist and family therapist, in my workshops with parents, teachers, and mental health professionals, and in the psychotherapy agency I direct.

Debra and Don recognized this gaping hole from their own personal experience as parents and partners, as well as decades' long practice working with families in their counseling center. Our world is filled with suggestions for change without any sense of a specific family's needs, or the bigger picture around the family, or why we apply the latest techniques, or why we still turn to certain techniques from decades ago. This is akin to doing surgery without conducting diagnostic procedures beforehand. None of us would ever think of a knee replacement without an x-ray, or consider removing a gallbladder without an MRI. But we are constantly bombarded with ideas to help us change our family relationships—those that matter so much to us—without first diagnosing what the problem is or where we need to focus.

In response, *How's Your Family Really Doing?* offers a simple yet comprehensive way to evaluate one's own family and identify both its strengths and areas for improvement. To accomplish this, the reader finds a fifty-point questionnaire. In a few minutes, one learns which of the *10 Keys to a Happy Loving Family* need more attention and exactly why. The chapters that follow outline ten foundational characteristics of healthy, happy families—one key at a time.

These chapters make immediate sense because they are presented in accessible language with case examples, practical suggestions, and personal anecdotes. Each summarizes "what we now know to be true," a phrase I use often in workshops. Debra and Don have dedicated enormous time and effort to separating myth from fact. They have synthesized what we know about families from longitudinal surveys, controlled research studies, the writings of key contributors to the field of psychology, parenting, and family systems, and, finally, their own work in the trenches with troubled families.

This important new reference provides an "all under one roof" opportunity to learn whatever you assess your own family needs to be. The average person would have to commit great resources in time and expense securing this specific kind of family relationship-assessment.

Now, if Don and Debra's contribution would stop here that would be enough. However, knowing the limitations of any one book, they've provided Self-Help Resources for each Key. This is done in order to take the reader deeper into areas that require attention and may change over time. For example, with young couples the Key #6, *Balancing Closeness and Distance* and Key #1, *Talking and Listening*, may be the most relevant; in the child-rearing years parents may well need more focus on Key #5, *Who's in Charge?* or Key #9, *Effective Problem Solving*. Later in the life cycle, Chapter 7 on *Accepting Differences* and Chapter 3, *Adapting to Change,* may become crucial.

These different, yet always accessible components inspired me to encourage Don and Debra to get this book out there. For me, as a father raising two kids with my wife Stacey—as a therapist for over thirty years—as someone who speaks nationwide to both parents and professionals—I am grateful to find a resource that describes family happiness, not as a vague concept, but as a set of specific, reachable goals that often change over time.

How's Your Family <u>Really</u> Doing? removes much of the confusion from our efforts to bring out the best in our families. It shows us how to construct a foundation of healthy habits, attitudes, and behaviors for more loving and effective family relationships. Debra and Don invite us to enjoy the process of self-discovery while offering genuine respect to use what fits with our own personal values.

How's Your Family <u>Really</u> Doing? offers basic tools to create happiness in family life upon which we can build a unique home, one in which we can live and love each other for many years to come—really!

-Ron Taffel, Ph.D., New York
Author of **Childhood Unbound** and **Breaking Through to Teens**

INTRODUCTION

We are one, after all, you and I; together we suffer, together exist, and forever will recreate each other.
-Teilhard de Chardin

When asked what they value most, the vast majority of people, male or female, young or old, married or single, say the same thing: family. However, as many of us know all too well, families can be like heaven or hell. They can lift us up or tear us apart. They can be our greatest refuge in difficult times or a source of unimaginable pain. Especially now. Especially here. Changes in the world are happening at breakneck speed, leaving us overwhelmed, overworked, and out of gas.

The idealized nuclear family with a stay-at-home mom is a thing of the past. According to *The Shriver Report* (The Center for American Progress, 2009), for the first time in America, women represent fifty percent of the workforce, and both parents work outside the home in two-thirds of all two-parent households. Unprecedented levels of stress and materialism, cultural shifts, and new technologies challenge the way we live. We need each other more than ever, yet have less time to spend with loved ones.

In our clinical practice we are also seeing problems that are new or greatly amplified: sexual activity and drug use in younger and younger children, Internet affairs, new and addictive forms of media engagement, an epidemic of childhood obesity, and record numbers of kids out of control. The list of difficulties and distractions goes on; families are under siege and desperate for help.

Since most people haven't had courses in how to be a family, our primary way of relating to each other has been determined by the families in which we grew up. Although we obviously don't want to recreate any unhealthy patterns from the families of our childhood, we often find ourselves lacking positive role models. Our parents did the best they could; yet they, too, had few alternatives to draw from and many suffered the emotional effects of their own upbringing. Even if they *had* searched for answers about family health and dysfunction from the most esteemed professionals of their day, good information on these issues was not readily available. Fortunately that information is now at our fingertips.

Although self-help books on parenting are as popular as ever, almost all have a particular focus on "the problem child," on addressing a particular parenting challenge, or on one developmental passage such as infancy, toddlerhood or adolescence. There are books on the explosive child, the out-of-sync child, the shy child, the overly sensitive child, and books that address sleep problems, disciplinary issues, and moral development. Although potentially useful, we have seen parents become frustrated or feel hopeless when they try new techniques at home with few successes. That's because these books fail to include the bigger picture of what might be happening in the family that contributes to the symptoms of the "problem child." Without focus on the essential threads that sustain health in the family as a whole, trying to help one person in isolation is often for naught.

As practicing psychotherapists for thirty plus years, we have sat with thousands of couples and families who have reached out for help. We have worked with clients presenting common complaints of everyday life as well as those with severe or chronic issues. In the formative years of our nonprofit, The Family Therapy Institute of Santa Barbara, we truly believed that the world would move from its penchant for focusing solely on the individual to recognizing and including the important information gleaned from what is called "family systems theory."

Simply put, psychotherapists trained in systems theory see the individual not in isolation but as an inseparable part of a dynamic whole. This approach integrates social, economic, and cultural information about the individual and examines each person within the context of his or her most significant relationships, both past and present. This larger lens is crucial. Rather than just zooming in on personal traits, a systems approach also focuses on how the individual relates to significant others—parents, siblings, children, friends, and their community and society as a whole. It is a positive, practical, strength-based approach.

We also incorporate findings from new research about the brain, which validate what family therapists have been saying for years, namely, that both positive and negative emotions are contagious. As this information emerged, we were certain that the link between the health and well-being of any child would be seen as dependent on the health and well-being of the family system. But still, even in our well-known family clinic, parents propose to drop off kids that they want us to fix without assessing the family's health first. For us, questioning whether family members impact one another is akin to asking whether the water affects the fish that are swimming in it.

The inspiration for this book came from several sources. As husband and wife and parents of two children, we share in the everyday struggle to "do it right." We strive to build intimacy into our family fiber, to keep communications lines open, and to handle conflict constructively. How do we know when things are off kilter? What can we do about it? These are questions we seek to answer for ourselves, our clients, and for our readers. As therapists working with diverse clients, we began to see patterns emerge. We discovered a foundation of core concepts that could be readily taught to help families be more successful and happy.

Finally, as teachers in graduate and postgraduate psychology programs, we were shocked to find how few students were being taught about what distinguishes healthy families from those that function poorly. Imagine the mistakes that we might have avoided had anyone taught us the means of healthy relating. Year after year our students have exclaimed, "Why didn't someone teach us this as a required course in high school?" Good question.

By burrowing through piles of professional literature and drawing on personal and professional experience, we have assembled what we believe to be the 10 Keys, or common factors, that can guide you toward building a happy loving family. Decades of research have demonstrated that families *can* successfully achieve the task of raising children who are able to live independently and establish stable and harmonious relationships. Families *can* create a sense of closeness, provide support and encouragement through times of stress, and yet still allow for the uniqueness of their members. Understanding the 10 Keys, you can make a tangible difference in your family that will last a lifetime.

This book begins with the **Current Family Assessment**, a fifty-point questionnaire that will help you pinpoint the strengths and areas for improvement in your personal relationships. The chapters that follow describe each of the 10 Keys. Through clinical anecdotes, personal examples and relevant psychological theory and research, we explain how each key can help unlock your potential for healthier functioning. Quotations by famous and not so famous people are scattered throughout to provide humor and poignancy. (It's amazing to see the wisdom of folks that didn't have the research to inform their opinions, but came to the same conclusions nonetheless.) Finally, we also include text boxes with an icon of a brain to entertain you with the latest tidbits of brain research that have practical implications for improving family relationships.

Once you have done the assessment, either by yourself or with other family members, and have read the chapters about each Key, you should have a pretty good answer for the big question: ***How's Your Family Really Doing?*** In the course of our practice, hundreds of families have read this material and used the process to great advantage. But we see this as only the beginning. This book can be used all over again as a checklist at critical developmental stages in the life of your family. The areas that need attention will inevitably change when you bond with a new partner or when the babies become young children, the children become teens, or after the nest is empty. Keep the book on the shelf as a reference, using the extensive bibliography to find important resources you will likely need along the way.

After examining each of the 10 Keys, the final part of the book discusses the process and pitfalls of making substantive changes in yourself and with your family. Chapter 11, Echoes of the Past, gives you another opportunity to be self reflective about how your childhood might be impacting your present challenges. The **Family of Origin Assessment** offers ways to examine the similarities and differences between your current family and your "family of origin" (the family you grew up in). Then you can consider whether or not you are making unwise compensations for your childhood experiences.

Chapter 12, Making Changes, outlines a variety of steps to engineer your process toward improvement. We offer concrete suggestions about how to initiate changes, how to include your children in the process, and what to do when you get stuck. Since we could never adequately address all of the potential problems and unique challenges that can make families stumble, we have endeavored to give you a trail guide to point you in the right direction. It is easy to get lost along the way, to get so mired down in the stresses of everyday life that potential solutions become obscured.

Making changes, even ones for the better, takes courage and commitment. Since you are reading this book, we figure that you are ready to examine how your relationships can be strengthened. Take your time, and try to enjoy the process. There is a lot of information to digest in the chapters that follow. Some of the tips and tools will appeal to you right away. Start with any small step towards change and build up from there. The journey to become more loving can only be taken one step at a time...

Our goals are to help you to:

- Understand the characteristics of healthy families and ways to bring out the best in each other.
- Identify the strengths and the areas for improvement for your family.
- Facilitate conversations between you, your partner, your parents, and children about desired changes.
- Create a working set of goals to focus your efforts at improvement.
- Examine the similarities and differences between your family of origin and your current family.
- Find specific ways to strengthen your skills in each of the
- ten areas using our "tips and tools," and/or other strategies
- and books listed under Self-Help Resources.
- In short, become a happier, healthier, more loving family!

A number of resources are also available at our website: **HowsYourFamily.com**. Included are copies of the Family Assessments, answers to frequently asked questions, tips and reminders for each of the 10 Keys, and a blog on current family topics.

For professionals such as teachers, therapists, pediatricians, and graduate students, we have established a special section on our website called Clinicians Corner. Included are guidelines for utilizing these materials with families. Please come and share your feedback, questions, and contributions.

GETTING STARTED

Begin by answering the fifty questions in the **Current Family Assessment** that follows. If you have a partner, a sibling, or an older child who wants to participate, make copies of the test and complete it independently of one another. Hold off on discussions and comparisons for now. Although younger children may not be able to take the test or understand certain things, we will instruct you later about how to include them in the process of assessment and change.

We have designed this assessment to work intimately with the content of the book, and there are five questions that relate to each Key. Go through and answer as honestly as you can. There are no "right" or "wrong" answers. The point is to identify both strengths and areas for improvement in your family.

Each item in the assessment describes a particular behavior or attitude that might or might not accurately describe your family. You are scoring each item based on your unique personal perspective. Decide what you believe to be true about your family right now. For most, the first step in any change process involves awareness. You will learn about elements of family functioning that you may not have thought about or put into words before.

Go to the next page now and take the test.

If you prefer, download free copies at
HowsYourFamily.com

Current Family Assessment

This assessment contains fifty statements, each describing a particular family strength. How much improvement do you believe your family needs on each item? Grade from 1–5 according to the following scale:

1	2	3	4	5
much need for improvement		some need for improvement		no need for improvement

Key #1

___ We talk things over and know what's going on with each other.

___ Individuals speak for themselves, not for others.

___ Each family member finds a balance between talking and listening.

___ We notice and discuss some of the nonverbal messages we send and receive.

___ We listen to one another's ideas or points of view.

___ Subtotal **Key #1**

Key #2

___ Feelings are expressed in a balanced way—not too much or too little.

___ We comfort one another and are able to cry openly when sad.

___ Feelings of fear, frustration, and anger can be shared constructively.

___ As needed, we use calming methods such as centering and slow deep breaths.

___ We share more positive feelings (joy, tenderness, pleasure) than negative ones (fighting, criticizing, yelling, teasing).

___ Subtotal **Key #2**

Key #3

___ We recognize and encourage each other's unique strengths.

___ Mistakes are treated as helpful learning opportunities.

___ We adapt well to losses, changes, and transitions.

___ We have developed good habits of exercise, self-care, and regular sleep.

___ Each of us draws social support from friends, extended family, and social groups.

___ Subtotal **Key #3**

Key #4

___ We like to spend time together.

___ There are established routines for bedtime, meals, and family time.

___ Family meals taken together occur more than once a week.

___ We have rituals that are special to our family and/or extended family.

___ Each family member spends some quality time with every other member.

___ Subtotal **Key #4**

Key #5

___ Parenting of the children is not too soft but not too strict.

___ The parental figures in our family are on the same page and work together.

___ We use encouragement and praise far more often than negative words.

___ Punishment consists of consequences rather than spanking or yelling.

___ The children follow rules and respect the adults as the leaders of the family.

___ Subtotal **Key #5**

Key #6

___ We find a balance between closeness and distance with each other.

___ We feel close and connected to other family members *and* to friends.

___ There is overall respect for each other's needs for independence.

___ Family members are usually available to one another for help and support.

___ We have "boundaries" that provide privacy between adults and children.

___ Subtotal **Key #6**

Key #7

___ Differences among family members are acknowledged and valued.

___ People don't "need to be right," allowing others to have their own perspective.

___ We acknowledge and accept differences in temperament and learning style.

___ Parents focus on the strengths of individual differences and teach tolerance.

___ As appropriate, we state preferences and requests rather than making demands.

___ Subtotal **Key #7**

Key #8

___ We emphasize the positive aspects of situations rather than complaining.

___ We teach about social values and moral decision-making.

___ We treat others the way we would like to be treated.

___ We are capable of offering apologies and being forgiving.

___ We emphasize spiritual values, the bigger picture in life, and service to others.

___ Subtotal **Key #8**

Key #9

___ We negotiate and compromise rather than one person dominating decision-making.

___ We face problems early on rather than waiting until things get out of hand.

___ Parents are organized and provide leadership to make decisions and follow through.

___ Family members feel respected for their ideas even when they don't get their way.

___ Children are included in decision-making in a way that is age appropriate.

___ Subtotal **Key #9**

Key #10

___ Parents provide a model of love, respect, and healthy boundaries.

___ Parents walk their talk rather than falling back on "Do as I say, not as I do."

___ Criticism and defensiveness happen infrequently as forms of communication.

___ Parents work towards agreement and keep conflict away from the children.

___ Parents make their relationship a priority, cultivating friendship and intimacy.

___ Subtotal **Key #10**

___ Total **Keys #1-10**

ANALYZING YOUR ASSESSMENT

Add up your scores for each of the individual Keys. The maximum score for each Key is 25 points, so a comparison of the point scores for each Key will clearly highlight your family's strengths and areas for growth. The first and most obvious starting point is to look at your present family's strengths and weaknesses. Examine your scores for each Key. Where did you score high? Where did you score poorly? If you have scored 16–25 on a Key, look on the component tested as a strength. If you scored from 12–15, the topics covered in this Key probably need some attention. A score from 5–11 identifies a problem Key. The results of this assessment will help you figure out how to obtain tangible results from this book. Circle your lowest scores and star those keys for later attention.

Next, compare the scores you gave your current family with those given by your partner or other family members. If there are big discrepancies, try to define what aspects of the Key led to differing conclusions. Listen to the perspectives of others and explain how you see things. Since there is no "right" answer, let it be okay to disagree. Bear in mind that each individual had a unique experience even while growing up in the same family. If you remain open and curious, you can learn a lot about each other just by comparing notes.

LEARNING ABOUT THE 10 KEYS

Now that you have completed your analysis, you can head in a few different directions. You can read the book from cover to cover, getting the big picture first, or you may be eager to learn about the areas that need the most improvement first. Since each of the 10 Keys is explained in detail in Chapters 1–10, you can turn immediately to the key that draws your attention, going back later to fill in the whole picture. We recommend that you read through all of the Keys at some point in your journey. Not only will you get a better understanding of each Key, you will also see how they interact with one another.

Key #1, Talking and Listening, and Key #2, Expressing Feelings, are particularly important. Most people need at least some brushing up in these areas, and some need major overhauls. Families rely on the skills and tools explained in these first two chapters to accomplish most of what follows.

Finally, after developing a more complete understanding of each Key, feel free to go back and reevaluate your answers. The book can be used like a workbook that allows you to chart your progress and make changes and notes as you go along. You'll be surprised how quickly you will learn how to make positive changes in yourself and your family simply by opening your mind, trying a few new tools, and keeping some pertinent tips in mind.

Since the book is intended to be a reference over the course of the lifetime of your family, use it like you might a favorite cookbook. Write notes in the margins. Dog-ear the pages that you want to come back to. Make copies of important points and put them on the refrigerator. Note the progress you are making and jot down the dates you take the assessment so you can look back at where you were.

Although the material that follows can be intense or seem like an overwhelming task, we invite you to see this process as an adventure. There will undoubtedly be both familiar and unfamiliar territory to explore. We hope that you will be able to laugh at some of your mistakes, just as we had to, and be gentle rather than judgmental when in new or uncomfortable terrain. Take your time.

CHAPTER ONE

KEY # 1
TALKING AND LISTENING

There is more than a grammatical tie between the words common, community, and communication....Try the experiment of communicating, with fullness and accuracy, some experience to another, especially if it is somewhat complicated, and you will find your own attitude toward your experience changing.
-John Dewey

*I*n thirty-five years of working with couples and families, some of the most common complaints that we hear are…

"We need tools to communicate better."
"He never talks to me!"
"I never know what she's thinking".
"I just can't talk to my parents…They don't listen to me."

Although in general we haven't put the 10 Keys in a specific order of importance, we have purposely put Talking and Listening first because of its universal significance. The presence of effective communication is one of the most frequently mentioned characteristics in the research on strong families. Without the ability to communicate, most of the information that follows in this book will be difficult, if not impossible, to implement. This chapter will look at only the most basic elements of healthy communication since entire books have been written on just this one topic.

Simply put, effective communication is the foundation of healthy relationships, thus underlying all of the other keys. It is the social thread that weaves us together. Depression and high conflict in families are almost always associated with difficulties people have talking and listening to one another. Low self-esteem can result from family members not speaking up about what they want, think, and feel. When we hold back from communicating, we are effectively saying to ourselves, "What I say and who I am doesn't count. I'm not important enough to be heard." The ability to express thoughts and feelings constructively is essential for healthy self-esteem. Nobody really wants to be talked down to. Everybody wants to be recognized. When we feel understood it helps us to be naturally more caring.

Communication in healthy families has some key characteristics: frequency, openness, honesty, and clarity. Quality dialogue includes a balance of talking and listening. Each member of the family does some of both. Try to encourage sharing events of the day as well as deeper thoughts, desires, and feelings. Daily conversation is at the crux of information flow in a family environment, the baseline for successful communication and inclusion.

Most people can use some help with communication tools. Training in effective communication is not a mandatory requirement before getting a marriage license. And most of us tend to think that the family patterns we grew up with are "normal." The other thing to bear in mind with this Key is that we can be good at communicating about some topics with some people but still not be able to communicate with our closest intimates about our deeper thoughts and feelings.

KEY ELEMENTS OF EFFECTIVE COMMUNICATION

Be sincere; be brief; be seated.
-Franklin D. Roosevelt

A good place to start is to remember to speak for yourself, not for others. While the concept is obvious you'd be surprised how many people have trouble speaking only on their own behalf. Notice the difference in clarity and tone when Mom says to the kids: "We don't need any more silly toys," instead of saying "I don't think we can afford that toy right now." Or perhaps a couple where the husband replies to his wife's request to go to a certain dinner place with, "No one likes that restaurant," instead of "I don't really like that place. Would it be okay if we went somewhere else?"

Another reminder is to keep communications reasonably brief, concise, and clear. You have probably noticed that people (particularly children) tune out a speaker who goes on and on and never gets to the point. Does anyone enjoy being lectured to? Sometimes when we work with couples where one person is getting more "air time" than the other, we bring the issue into focus by having each person speak for a few sentences and stop and give the other person a turn.

Consider how you might feel about these two different ways that someone spoke to you: "You never pick up your room," as opposed to, "It really bugs me that you haven't picked up your room in a while. Please do it now." Or another example: "You are always late for everything!" when the alternative might be. "I really don't want to be late for this event. Please be back in time," or "I'm going to go on ahead." Observe that the second examples in these exchanges include the element of speaking for yourself, what we therapists call using an "I" message." We will describe the use of this technique later in this chapter when we discuss the "Repair Kit."

Try to avoid the use of absolutes. Words like "never," "always," and "every time," particularly when they are used while lodging a complaint about something or someone else, tend to be either conversation stoppers or ways to begin a fight. The most typical response to being told that we "never listen" or "always leave the kitchen a mess," is to be instantly defensive. We are more likely to follow up with an equivalent charge about how the other person never talks to us, or always leaves the bathroom towels on the floor.

YOU CAN'T TALK AND LISTEN AT THE SAME TIME

If speaking is silver, then listening is gold.
-Turkish proverb

Besides learning to talk in positive ways, mastering the skill of good listening is critical to quality communication and probably the more difficult of the two. Just as with excessive and negative talking, many of us get into the bad habit of not really listening.

Do you truly listen to your friends and family members? Do you feel heard?

As testimony to the importance of the simple act of listening, we regularly have clients who walk into our office with a smile, sit down, and start to cry as they begin to talk. "Why do I always cry when I come here? I don't even feel sad," Mary sniffs apologetically. We'll respond by saying, "It might be because you've learned that whatever you share, I will really listen to you." Often these are tears not only of relief but of gratitude.

So what are the tools for effective listening? A good listener is patient, calm, and centered, provides eye contact, sits quietly, and sometimes provides touch. Effective listening takes effort and practice. One contribution might be eliminating TV, radio, computer, or cell phone interruptions that take attention away from the speaker. Also helpful is the listener's participation with what are called "minimal encouragers," little words like "really" or "uh-huh" or "wow" or "tell me more." These expressions let the speaker know that you are tuned in. A good listener asks open questions or inquires to get more details ("What happened next?" or "When did this happen?" or "How did that feel?")

Try to pay attention rather than drifting into your own thoughts or feelings. Many people, instead of listening without judgment, fall into a pattern of formulating their own response or defense to what's being said. Instead of really "hearing" what their loved one is going through or feeling, they respond and act a bit like lawyers in a courtroom battle.

In one typical scenario, Susan begins telling her husband Larry about a fight she had with their teenage son. She gets out a few sentences and he says, "What did you do to get him so pissed off?" or "Why did you do that!" Instantly Susan gets defensive and walks away angry, feeling Larry never even listened to what happened before he responded with upset. In another scenario, Larry shares how much he misses intimate contact with his wife. Susan jumps in before he finishes to explain how many things she had to do that day. Larry's face drops. Sound familiar?

A speaker knows that he's been heard if the listener repeats back what's been said, but in her own words. This technique, called active listening, is another important tool that we teach our clients. In order to ensure that you truly understand what the other person means, repeat back the essence of what you heard and then confirm by saying something like "Is this what you meant?"

In the example of the case of Susan and Larry, the discussion would have been more productive if Larry had listened and then said something like, "It sounds like you are really upset about your argument. Tell me what happened next?" An empathetic approach opens up the conversation as well as making Susan feel that her husband has some understanding of her pain about their son. In the example of Larry's complaint, Susan might have used active listening and said, "It sounds like you miss spending time with me...Is that what's troubling you?" Larry then has the opportunity to clarify what was said or say more about what he is missing. Many misunderstandings can be nipped in the bud by working toward more clarity with these tools.

To be honest, my own personal style can often be a bit too blunt, sometimes blurting out what I think or feel. Working with couples, I often share that this "stuff" about communication that I'm teaching them can difficult to apply. I often say, "I'd much rather not have to edit how I express feelings. It's hard to listen, too, so when I'm not monitoring myself I can easily check out. But even though it can be a real pain in the butt for an impatient guy like me, I keep using these tools because they really work." –Don

THE IMPORTANCE OF NONVERBAL COMMUNICATION

One cannot not communicate.
-Paul Watzlawick

Communication also includes messages not conveyed in words. In order to have effective interactions with family members, it really helps to understand the nonverbal signals that accompany our words. Most studies have shown that a whopping sixty percent of the messages we send are nonverbal (Birdwhistell, 1970), making it the single most powerful form of communication. More than intonation or even words, nonverbal communication can provide clues to what is going on inside the other person.

Nonverbal communication includes a number of elements in addition to facial expressions. These include tone of voice, volume, and the inflections applied to words. Also important are forms of body language—all the things done with the rest of the body while talking, such as crossing arms or legs, wiggling, pacing, etc. Another nonverbal clue is the amount of distance between the speaker and the listener. Doesn't it feel different to talk to someone who is yelling at you from another room versus having a conversation while sitting together on the couch?

An additional element is the focus of our eyes; principally whether we look at one another or look away. Whether or not we engage someone with eye contact also sends a message. Each person is unique in just how much or how little eye contact feels comfortable or polite. We also unwittingly communicate or receive communications differently depending on how and whether we are touching during the conversation. All of these things play an enormous role in the messages we are constantly sending and receiving. To complicate matters further, many of these nonverbal cues can be sent and received unconsciously rather than deliberately.

Yet another wrinkle in this complex process is how the "rules" of polite communication vary greatly in different cultures, in different social classes, and in different families. Conversations between males and females or between children and adults may have additional prohibitions. Not so long ago it was a common admonishment that "Children are to be seen and not heard." Given all these potential variations our body language, facial expressions, use of space, and especially gestures, are highly vulnerable to misinterpretation and are often at the core of misunderstandings.

A couple came into therapy to receive help about their conflict with one another. He was from Kansas and she was from Mexico. Two very different people in lots of ways, she was pretty laid back while he described himself as rigid. They were both bilingual. She spoke Spanish to him and he responded in English. One of the

---

earlier issues in their relationship was that she'd promise to do things "mañana," which he took quite literally to mean "tomorrow." Her use of the word only meant "sometime in the future." It took them months, even after they realized the nature of their misunderstanding, to work out the feelings related to this communication mismatch.

Although misunderstandings can arise from words alone, we also often misread nonverbal signals. Confusion is inevitable when someone's verbal message does not match the nonverbal signals. All of us have been both victim and perpetrator of these complicated mixed messages. We often marvel to clients how it is quite miraculous, when you examine the complexity of communication, that we ever understand each other at all!

IMPROVING NONVERBAL COMMUNICATION

Families break up when people take hints you don't intend and miss hints you do intend.
-Robert Frost

Some people have a knack for using nonverbal communication effectively and for correctly interpreting signals from others. Paying careful attention to nonverbal behavior and practicing different types of nonverbal communication with others can build this skill. Just as with talking and listening, understanding nonverbal communication can improve with practice. The first step is to recognize its importance.

Remember that you are constantly communicating with your face, voice tone, and body even more than with your words. Make a practice of noticing how you sound, how tense or relaxed you are...especially if your partner or kids keep responding to you as if you are upset. They may be seeing cues that you are unaware of sending.

When you are in an important conversation, especially when feelings are involved, be sure to watch facial expressions, eye contact, posture, hand and feet movements, body movement, and placement. Ask yourself, what is being said without words? Let's say that your daughter comes home from school and tells you how much she hates her teacher, but from looking at her face it appears that she is sad and hurt. Instead of saying, "There's no reason to hate your teacher. She's a nice lady," you might offer, "You look really sad, like she hurt your feelings." You can see how a whole different conversation may then take place.

Also important, as illustrated by the example just given, is the practice of checking out our assumptions. Many arguments can be avoided by using this simple tool. Couples often think they know what their partner is feeling but fail to take the time to confirm their perceptions. One way to test your ability is to see if you can guess what another person is feeling (happy, sad, scared, frustrated, embarrassed, etc). After that, check with the other person to see if you are accurate or not.

Often you will find that a person's words say one thing and their nonverbal communication says something completely different. Our advice is to "listen" to the nonverbal communication first. Check out what you are seeing, e.g. "You are saying you are happy but your face looks sad when you talk about your work. Is everything okay?" This is a time when you can usually trust your gut. All of us have had gut feelings at times about whether to trust or not to trust someone's communication and later, have wished that we had listened to our instincts. Your gut feelings, along with your life experiences, training, and beliefs shape your inner receiver and sender of nonverbal communication.

Bear in mind that a single gesture or look might mean any number of things or nothing at all. One way to read nonverbal behavior is to look for groups of signals that reinforce a common point. Don't place too much emphasis on just one signal out of many, but look for the pieces of a complete picture. A person's overall demeanor is far more telling than a single gesture viewed in isolation.

Research on empathic accuracy (Gleason, et al., 2009) has shown that some children exhibit what might be described as a nonverbal learning disability because they are so unable to interpret messages that others are sending. Some bullies, for example, misread the signs of fear in the faces of other kids, attacking because of what they perceive as signs of anger instead. Other kids are oblivious to the negative reactions of others when they get too close, nose up to them, and invade their personal space. They often end up being shunned by their peers and not understanding why.

A final point to remember is to factor in the situation and context in which any given communication occurs. Some situations require more formal behaviors that might be interpreted very differently in another setting. Consider whether or not nonverbal behaviors are appropriate for the context. People live by varying rules of etiquette. Your mother-in-law may deny being angry when out to dinner but be willing to talk about it later in private.

THE GIFT OF UNDERSTANDING

Studies show that people report greater life satisfaction and fewer physical symptoms on the exact days when they feel more understood by others in verbal interactions (Lun, et al., 2008). Neuroscientists explain that when people feel heard and understood, their emotional brains settle down in a way that is almost miraculous...similar to a car on the freeway that is stuck in second gear and suddenly shifts into fifth... *Ahhhhh*....

TIPS AND TOOLS FOR COMMUNICATION

I remind myself every morning: Nothing I say this day will teach me anything. So if I'm going to learn, I must do it by listening.
-Larry King

There are a few rules that we often repeat as therapists. So often, even good communicators mess up because their timing is off. *Make a conscious effort to choose the appropriate time and place to talk,* especially when addressing important or emotionally charged subject matter. Avoid "hot topics" when family members are tired, hungry, "under the influence," or when there really isn't enough time to handle the issue (i.e. right before someone has to be at work or just before going to bed). Most of us feel disrespected and get off to a bad start when an emotionally charged issue is brought up when we're otherwise preoccupied. A good example of a fight waiting to happen is to bring up a charged issue when your spouse has just walked in the door from work, when your teen is immersed in a conversation with a friend, or when your partner has just concluded a disturbing professional or personal phone call.

For this reason and especially for heavier topics, we encourage family members to make an "appointment" with one another for the conversation. A good beginning might be, "I have something that I would like to talk to you about. Would this be a good time?" If it's not a good time, the person who has been approached can offer a time soon after when they *are* available. Often the person anxious to talk right away will justify bursting instantly into conversation (even at a really bad time) by complaining that there "will never be a good time." To avoid this particular scenario, the best practice is for the more reluctant partner to make a firm commitment to be available at a later time and place.

Consider creating new agreements or rituals when trying to break old bad habits. A technique that works for many couples is to *establish a special "spot"* (such as a certain set of chairs) so that there is a new setting in which to practice new behavior. When families have had lots of conflict, they'll often associate certain rooms or places at home with the old bad habits of communication. A new place can help to break the old mold. Start with simple sharing about your day until you are more skilled at talking and listening. All of us learn better when we are not upset, so it's helpful to practice first with lighter topics rather than pulling out the big guns right away.

Take care as you pick your time and place since *topics such as sex and money and/or yelling or intense conflict are not good for "little ears."* If you anticipate that the discussion may be heated, save it for when the kids are at school or asleep. Better yet, make a date and time for conversations such as these. You will be more successful when emotions have cooled and all parties have had some time to reflect rather than react.

The Repair Kit for Sharing Feelings and Conflict Resolution

The "repair kit" is equally helpful with adults and kids alike. Couples can use these tools to practice new skills for both talking and listening, and can become effective at coaching their kids in the process.

Person #1 starts as the speaker, and person #2 as the listener, and they are positioned to sit face to face so knees are almost touching. Deep breaths are suggested to help the listener from becoming anxious or defensive. Person #1 shares with person #2 each of the following:

1. A genuine appreciation toward the other.
2. Something he or she is upset about. Examples: "It made me mad when you teased me about my shirt today." "I didn't like it when…." "I don't like it when…"
3. A wish or a want that would help fix the thing the person is upset about. Examples: "I want you to be nice to me and not tease." "I would appreciate it if you wouldn't do that."

After sharing one way, the flow reverses so that person #1 becomes the listener and person #2 becomes the speaker. Participants should also pause to take deep breaths while reversing roles. Breathing consciously is one of the fastest and most effective de-stressors available…

The "repair kit" can be used effectively with kids as young as five or six. When you first introduce the exercise, you may want to share that Mom and Dad have been trying something new that is helping them get along better. First practice this tool with kids as part of a family meeting, when things are going well. Explain that, "We know that broken things such as a flat tire need repair. We also have learned that when people aren't acting in caring ways toward each other, something needs fixing." Model how to do it and then have each one build their skills by initially "pretending" to be upset with the other about something. This process can be used for family bickering as often as a few times a week to help things run more smoothly. Kids usually need coaching in their efforts even after the "repair kit" is learned.

To summarize the essence of the first Key...we can't overemphasize the importance of healthy communication. *In happy, loving families, family members take time to check in and talk and listen to one another.* As hard as connecting can be in the hurried pace of our day-to-day lives, quality communication is more important than ever. Families do best when they have ritualized times to talk together. They make a habit of talking at family dinners, even if they can't be together every night. Couples plan weekly date nights or lunch meetings. Outings can be arranged on weekends or days off. Bedtime rituals allow time for talking and connecting before dozing off.

Remember that the frequency of communication contributes to the closeness that we all long for in families. Without it, we lose touch with each other's thoughts, feelings, and dreams. We become lonely and isolated. We are, after all, meant to be part of a tribe, and to feel like a tribe we must talk and listen to one another. Since so much rests on your ability to communicate, you might even want to evaluate this Key more fully by taping a family discussion and have each member write down what they perceive as strengths and shortcomings in that conversation.

Now that you better understand the nature of this Key, you may want to go back and re-score yourself in the Current Family Assessment.

KEY #1 TIPS: TALKING AND LISTENING

- Find a balance between talking and listening.
- Speak only for yourself, not for others.
- Avoid the use of words that are absolutes such as "never" and "always."
- Notice and discuss some of the nonverbal messages you send and receive.
- Practice the use of "I" messages.
- Keep communications reasonably brief, concise, and clear.

CHAPTER TWO

KEY # 2
EXPRESSING FEELINGS

*There can be no transforming of darkness into light
and of apathy into movement without emotion.*
-Carl Jung

*T*here are lots of ways that feelings can be expressed in families. In the first chapter we addressed verbal and nonverbal communication. In this chapter we will also focus on ways to help family harmony by expressing our feelings with other family members, as well as on our own. We will talk about all kinds of feelings, those considered "positive" such as love, joy and appreciation as well as those considered "negative" such as anger, sadness, fear, grief or embarrassment. They all play an important role. Studies suggest that we can even heal more rapidly from physical injury and pain when we express ourselves through laughter, tears, and shaking rather than holding our feelings in. By the way, you're in for a special treat. This chapter is plastered with a variety of metaphors to describe feelings and healing processes. Choose the ones that work for you and forget the rest!

Before being able to express feelings or have the ability to empathize with others, first we have to become aware of them inside of ourselves. Just cultivating awareness of what is going on—naming the sensations without judgment and without pushing them away can be the beginning of healing. Often our bodies give us clues to what we might be experiencing. For example, angry feelings are often stored with tension in the jaw, back, shoulders, and/or neck. Sometimes as a first step (but only if offered in a caring manner), family members can also reflect back to us what they think we might be feeling by how we look. **Healthy families are able to express feelings constructively, striking a balance between holding too much in and letting too much out.** When communicated in non-blaming ways, both positive and negative feelings can build greater understanding and intimacy. When people hold feelings inside, they can develop symptoms of depression and low self-esteem. There is also a greater tendency to display psychosomatic symptoms such as stomachaches, bedwetting, gastrointestinal problems, rashes, headaches, etc. Holding feelings inside also can lead to passive-aggressive (meaning indirect) expressions of those feelings somewhere down the line. Examples of such behavior include withdrawing from others, becoming stubborn, teasing, or using sarcasm.

I love to tell the story of my inability to express anger directly when I was in my twenties. Angry feelings weren't allowed in my family. My dad's way of supposedly not being angry was to retreat into the garage and fix bicycles. No surprise that when I was in my first steady relationship in college, I withdrew and became a bit passive-aggressive when I was upset with my girlfriend. I even ran off into the woods and hid behind a tree, secretly wishing she'd come find me and drag my feelings out. –Don

Perhaps one of the best metaphors for not letting feelings out is to think about "kitchen garbage." If you let a bunch of chicken bones and soup cans sit around too long without taking the garbage out, things start to stink up a bit. The same can be true with feelings. They need to come out and you need to let them out. It's not that they are given huge importance or demand our attention all the time, but that they simply want to get expressed.

At the opposite extreme are families where there is a loss of control of emotions or too much weight placed on their meaning or importance. Negative feelings in such families are typically expressed in a destructive fashion rather than resolved by good listening or channeled constructively. Not much gets accomplished when there's emotional chaos and feelings are flying all over the place.

Many people believe in the myth that the more feelings you share, the better your marriage or family will be, or the closer you'll feel. That may be true for positive feelings, but not necessarily for negative ones. Some people say, "Well, I'm just being honest and telling it like it is! Shouldn't a person be one-hundred-percent honest?" No, it obviously doesn't help closeness for people to be "dumping" on each other with their most honest and uncensored feelings.

Expressing feelings in constructive ways is good for our relationships, and for our bodies. Another useful concept is to think of "learning how to have your hand on the faucet of your feelings," to be able to open the faucet when you want to with a safe person who will support you in your release, but also keep the faucet from flowing with anger or tears when it isn't the right time or place. This form of emotional "self-regulation" is a high predictor of how we get along with others in general.

WHY WE HAVE EMOTIONS

The happiness of a man in this life does not consist in the absence but in the mastery of his passions.
-Alfred Lord Tennyson

Before we explore more about this second Key, it's helpful to understand some essential elements of our emotional landscape. What are emotions for? Where do they come from? How do they relate to thinking? Why are they so important? Wouldn't we all be better off without them? To answer these questions, we have to dig into what we know about how the brain works.

One of the early pioneers interested in emotions was Charles Darwin. In his travels he observed that people everywhere have certain common facial expressions (a smile, a frown, a furrowed brow) and that they represent a universal language of sorts. He also hypothesized that emotions are crucial to survival. Recent brain imaging studies have confirmed this fact.

Although there are hundreds of kinds of feelings, there are certain primary or essential emotions that can be recognized across cultures. These are anger, sadness, fear, hurt, enjoyment, love, surprise, disgust, and shame. Each of these primary emotions serves an important function.

THE EMOTIONAL MIND

The emotional mind is like a radar system that tries to protect us from harm and aims us in the right direction. When we sense danger, our emotions allow us to react before we even think. When we sense something we need (food, comfort) our feelings tell us which way to go. They are absolutely essential in helping us make good decisions. How we deal with them also has important implications for how to have a happy loving family.

 AMYGDALA HIJACKINGS

The seat of emotions is in the old part of the brain called the limbic system. A key structure in this area is the amygdala, a powerful contributor to our thoughts and feelings, although only the size and shape of an almond. A pioneering neuroscientist, Joseph LeDoux (1998), showed how the amygdala, as the emotional watchdog, can literally take control over our body in a heartbeat. When we see or hear something that triggers strong fear, the amygdala reacts instantaneously and we act before we're able to think. Daniel Goleman, in his bestseller *Emotional Intelligence*, aptly and creatively named this "an amygdala hijacking." The amygdala takes over the driver's seat and directs us to do something we didn't consciously decide to do, for better or for worse.

It might seem odd, but we explain these elements of brain science to almost every client. We go through this mini-lecture for two important reasons. First, although these hijackings happen to everyone at times, for some they can be highly debilitating. For people with chronic stress—those living in war zones, abusive relationships, unsafe neighborhoods, or with chronic pain—the limbic system can be triggered multiple times each day or hour. Second, this arousal of the emotional brain, especially when mishandled or misunderstood, can wreak havoc in relationships.

THE FIGHT-FLIGHT-FREEZE RESPONSE

Most of us have had this experience before. We're about to take a step off a curb and a car seems to appear out of nowhere. In a split second our reflexes kick in and we grab our child's hand and jump backwards. Our hearts continue to pound for a few seconds. Although we never had a moment to think, our amygdala hijacking served its goal of preserving our life.

Many years ago, I found myself in our sons' bedroom in the middle of the night while an earthquake was still shaking the house. I had gotten there safely without knowing why or how, and then realized what was happening. Only later, when out of shock, did the feelings of fear wash over me. This experience taught me how helpful our built-in reflexes can be. –Debra

When the amygdala takes over, there are three responses available in an instant: fight, flight, or freeze. When the saber-toothed tiger attacked in our prehistoric history, we stood up to fight back, ran like hell, or froze like a rabbit. In modern times we still do the same thing. Only now, much to our chagrin, sometimes the response is to our husband rather than a tiger.

We find it useful to ask people what their typical response is when emotional instinct takes over. Quite often, men's first response is fight followed by flight. Women tend toward flight or freeze followed by fight. Couples talking about an event that prompted an amygdala hijacking are often judgmental. "Why didn't you run?" or "Why did you snap at me?" or, "Why didn't you yell for help?" The answer to all these questions is, "Just because." We are each wired up to respond the way that we do. It's difficult to stop our own reactions because we are unable to really *think* when the amygdala takes over.

What we experience as threatening can differ greatly from one person to the next. Although there are many universal fears (like the car swerving, a strange intruder, a growling, teeth-baring dog, etc.) there are also fear reactions that are highly individualized or learned. Most of this learning has been wired into us by the time we are seven years old. We often have no conscious memory of what triggers our fears, but our amygdala responds just the same.

Any event can get unconsciously interpreted as a sign of danger when something in the present moment reminds the amygdala of past upset. This explains why, particularly in moments of intense emotion, people can do or say things they would never do otherwise.

EMOTIONAL "FLOODING"

Feelings are what connect us to life and to one another. To be able to feel is one of the extraordinary gifts of humanity. To neither suppress our feelings nor be caught by them but to withstand them, that is the art.
-Jack Kornfield

How we handle our amygdalas and emotions obviously influences our ability to resolve conflict with loved ones. John Gottman, one of America's foremost researchers on healthy marriages, coined the word "emotional flooding" in *What Predicts Divorce* (1994) to describe what is essentially an amygdala hijacking triggered by interpersonal conflict. Have you ever noticed, when in a heated discussion, your heart thumping, your pulse racing, your blood pressure rising, your face flushing, and your hands or body sweating? This uncomfortable set of sensations makes it almost impossible to listen, think, and/or react rationally. The body surges with adrenalin and other stress related hormones, going into fight or flight mode.

All of these reactions can develop with just a few minutes of arguing; they might not emerge for an hour; they might not happen at all for some very calm individuals. But when the flood rises, watch out! Just as storm waters can rush over the banks of a river causing horrible destruction, so too can emotionally overwhelmed people cause irreparable damage to a relationship. Too much expression of emotion in these moments can yield enormous interpersonal wreckage.

What makes things more difficult is that often you can't tell simply by observing someone that they are flooded. The person experiencing emotional overload is not necessarily the person who is yelling the loudest. The best method for checking your condition is to stop and take your pulse. If it is beating eighteen times a minute higher than your resting heart rate then you are "flooded." Your body is armed and ready for mortal combat (biologically speaking).

You experience that your mate or teenager is a threatening animal about to attack, and you are ready to say or do anything to survive.

One of the more surprising findings in Gottman's research is that men and women typically have different abilities to handle stressful encounters. When compared to women, men tend to experience flooding much sooner and are also challenged by the fact that they have more difficulty calming back down.

As far as families are concerned, moms and dads can be equally challenged. Parenting provides plenty of opportunities to learn to deal with our amygdalas, and echoes of strong emotions can sometimes last for hours. Here is a typical example.

Roger and Julie were a couple from a blended family. Roger got upset when he noticed his fourteen-year-old daughter wearing a sexy spaghetti-strapped blouse as she was headed off to school. She was well developed for her age and her dad was uncomfortable with the way she was revealing herself.

After yelling at his daughter in the driveway in front of all the neighbors, Roger continued to be "swamped" with emotions for the next twelve hours. Even though his wife approached him a number of times to talk about it, he denied having any feelings. Nevertheless he berated her over the fact that the knob on the washing machine had broken, snapped at his son about a homework issue, and yelled at his friend on the phone. Fortunately, by the time of our session, he had calmed down and could laugh at the many things that he found to be upset about after the "spaghetti strap crisis."

Although his concern about his daughter may have been valid, it took Roger, by his own admission, way too long to settle down, and in the meantime he had been a seething bundle of emotions looking for justification. When we have "big feelings," we can find all kinds of reasons to be upset with things going on around us. The brain searches its immediate environment to find an explanation for its emotional activation, essentially hunting for a person or situation to blame.

TIPS & TOOLS ABOUT "FLOODING"

The real art of conversation is not only to say the right thing at the right place but to leave unsaid the wrong thing at the tempting moment.
-Dorothy Nevill

If family discussions routinely turn into arguments, consider calling for a timeout. Make the referee "T" sign with your hands. Respecting the need for a timeout has to be nonnegotiable. No one should be blamed for the body's reaction under stress. If a family member says they need a timeout, give it to them. But after the break, rather than hanging the other person up for days, it's only fair that "within a reasonable period of time" the person who was flooded should approach the other to finish the healing conversation so that there can be resolution.

Although many couples believe that you should never go to bed angry, there *are* times when feelings are just too hot to handle. Agree ahead of time to take a break if emotions get high. Trying to talk something through to a good conclusion when one or both participants are really upset cannot only be futile but can be downright damaging. Sometimes it's better to continue the discussion in the morning when heads are cooler or when no one is under the influence of drugs or alcohol. Otherwise it can make things worse.

It can take twenty to thirty minutes to get the pulse rate back to normal and regain a clear head. If you are not practiced at stopping negative thoughts and calming yourself, it can take hours. Many people find that taking some private space to run around the block, pound a hard pillow or bed, or scream profanities into a towel and then take lots of sighs and long slow deep breaths can make the recovery process quicker and more effective. These exercises serve the body by reducing the levels of cortisol and adrenalin, two hormones that feed our highly activated state. We will discuss these methods in more detail later in this chapter.

WHAT ARE MY REAL FEELINGS?

One more note about flooding: All of us (the authors included) say things while flooded that make us feel embarrassed, guilty, or shocked at ourselves or our partner. Do you know anyone who hasn't at times said something ridiculous or out of control? We've heard clients say: "I wish I had never married you!" "Why don't you go jump off a bridge!" or "Why don't you go live with your father—you're just like him!" We also receive frantic phone calls from parents when their kids have said, "You're the worst mother in the world!" "I hate you!" or "I wish I was never born!"

Some people have the belief that words spoken in anger are "the real truth" and replay them over and over in their heads. This notion that what we say "under fire" is our deep hidden reality cannot be further from the truth. Usually the best explanation is that our expressions are a sign of being overwhelmed and the best that we could do at the time. They are spewed by the part of our brain that is in a biological battle for survival. We react like a trapped animal in the corner. (Even sweet beloved pets will bite when terrified.) To be happy and loving, we can all learn better ways to take responsibility and manage these feelings. In the meantime, try not to judge yourself, your partner or your child for "flooded words."

DIFFERENCES IN EXPRESSION: THE ROLE OF CULTURE, GENDER AND TEMPERAMENT

Although the existence of emotions crosses all racial, gender, and cultural lines, there are vast differences in how openly each of us expresses our feelings. We are each taught in our culture and family of origin which feelings we are supposed to show publicly and which we are supposed to hide or hold back. In some families, children are not allowed to express anger at their parents. In others, boys aren't allowed to cry but girls are. There are cultures where heterosexual men can walk down the street holding hands and others where touching in public is forbidden.

When a couple marries and they are from different social class, racial or ethnic backgrounds, they often struggle with the effects of vastly different rules or practices about sharing their feelings. In those instances a couple will ideally explore and become more familiar with the emotional legacy that one party or the other has brought to the marriage and what new rules should apply in the newly created family.

We have also learned about the role of inborn traits and differences in temperament that can be observed from infancy on. So many behavioral differences between children that used to be blamed on poor parenting are now seen as genetically determined. We will address this issue and describe the different temperaments in Chapter 7. For now, remember that some people inherently have bigger feelings than others.

EMOTIONAL INTELLIGENCE

Dan Goleman's book *Emotional Intelligence: Why It Can Matter More Than IQ* brought the idea and importance of "EQ" to the forefront in 1995. Previous research had looked at more traditional measures of intelligence, or IQ, to try to predict success in school, work, and relationships. We now realize that emotional intelligence is a better predictor of success and happiness in life than IQ. The five main characteristics of emotional intelligence are:

- Emotional self-awareness: the ability to recognize and name feelings as they are happening and understand their causes.
- Managing emotions: the ability to tolerate frustration and control anger appropriately and develop positive feelings.
- Harnessing emotions constructively: the ability to delay instant gratification and tolerate frustration as we reach toward our goals.
- Empathy: the ability to recognize emotions of others, listen, and be understanding.
- Handling relationships: the ability to resolve conflict and solve problems in a relationship, use good communication tools, and be more cooperative and helpful.

THE VALUE OF BOTH POSITIVE AND NEGATIVE EMOTIONS

As you now understand from our quick study of brain science, emotions have evolved and persisted for important reasons. They really serve us when viewed from a survival perspective. However, there is a great deal of research on the fact that becoming mired in negative mood states cannot only be unpleasant for yourself and others but can contribute to physical problems such as heart disease, depression, and autoimmune disorders. Conversely, a consistently healthy emotional state can contribute to greater longevity. A study at Harvard Medical School (Mittleman, et al., 1995) found that the emotion most commonly occurring two hours prior to heart attacks is anger, and that once someone has heart disease, a state of continuing anger can be particularly lethal. Another study (Kubansky, et al., 2001) followed optimistic and pessimistic people for thirty years and found that pessimists consistently developed more serious diseases. Clearly, finding a way to move through more distressing emotions is like the old apple-a-day: it keeps the doctor away.

Avoiding negative emotions by denying or repressing them doesn't help either. Some studies (Pennebaker & Traue, 1993) have looked at individuals who are considered feeling "repressors." Despite saying they are not feeling tense, these individuals can be identified with biofeedback machines that measure tension and minor facial expressions. The data suggests that repressors are more susceptible to diseases like asthma, high blood pressure, and viruses. We also know that when people ignore their anger and their grief, they can grow more and more embittered, disconnected from others and vengeful. Repressed anger can turn to withdrawal, violence, or hatred; and untended sorrow can lead to depression, anxiety, and addictions.

Everything points to the same conclusion. Feelings are helpful messages about what we like and don't like, what is or isn't working in our lives, and what we should approach or avoid. A helpful path is to get the message, feel the feeling, and then move on to clear thinking and appropriate action when needed. As Antonio Damasio (1999), one of the leading scientists in this field, explains, "The neurological evidence simply suggests that selective absence of emotion is a problem. Well-targeted and well-deployed emotion seems to be a support system without which the edifice of reason cannot operate properly." As psychotherapists we are heartened to have brain scientists confirm what we have known and practiced intuitively all along.

THE ROLE OF POSITIVE EMOTIONS

One can overcome the forces of negative emotions, like anger and hatred, by cultivating their counter forces, like love and compassion.
-Dalai Lama

Interestingly, much less attention has been paid until recently to the positive side of the equation. We know that excitement fuels curiosity, fostering new learning, creativity, and exploration. Love, which seems to be a collection of a number of positive feelings, is essential to building the bonds of family, friendship, and community. We now know that engaging in new behaviors activates brain growth. What better way to activate your brain than the feelings of pleasure or the joy of laughter?

Positive emotions help us to overcome negative ones (Frederickson, et al., 2000). They can assist us in letting go of anger, sadness, and fear, and to move away from a potential downward spiral that leads to more negativity. Individuals who express higher levels of positive emotion also show more constructive thinking and flexible coping skills. They are better able to think about the future and create helpful emotional distance after stressful events. When people can find something positive in loss, seeing the silver lining in the dark cloud, they are less distressed a year later than those who lack the healing function of the positive emotions.

Happy, loving families also share more positives like appreciation, tenderness, favors, acts of caring, consideration, smiles, and nurturing physical touch. In fact, *research shows that it's best to create a ratio of 5:1 positive to negative interactions to keep a relationship feeling close and connected* (Gottman, 1994). Even in couples with high levels of expressed conflict, if the ratio is 5:1 these couples fare well in the long run. For some of you this may seem like an overwhelming task, and it may take time and practice over many weeks to achieve this ratio, but every step in that direction is well worth the effort.

In sum, positive communications create a warm, loving atmosphere. Within this safe context and utilizing good communication skills, talking about negative feelings in families helps to bring deeper understanding and closeness.

TIPS & TOOLS FOR CRYING WHEN YOU WANT TO

When grief is fresh, every attempt to divert only irritates. You must wait till it be digested, and then amusement will dissipate the remains of it.
-Samuel Johnson

We began this chapter by explaining that individuals in healthy families feel safe to express feelings with one another, finding a balance between too much and too little expression. Some people cry easily and others don't, largely due to social conditioning. There are certain circumstances where people cry to get what they want and use tears manipulatively; but ruling this out, expression of feelings can facilitate healing.

A genuine release through crying is the healing of pain, and so should be supported. Haven't you had a friend tell you how much she felt better after a "good cry?" Crying fully when we need to can bring relief as well as return us to the present moment. After this release we naturally become more "accepting" of what is. As one client said, "It can be like the clearing of the sky after a thunderstorm!"

When we say "crying," we don't mean just watery eyes or quickly wiping away tears before they get half way down your cheeks. Have you ever watched a young child cry? Given the opportunity they'll do it with one hundred percent of their being, no holds barred, turning beet red and breaking into a sweat. There are sobs, moans, slobbering and movements of the tummy. When the expression is complete, they stop as quickly as they started and smile contentedly again. You, too, were able to cry like this as a child until perhaps you got "socialized" out of it. Many adults pretend that they don't feel, hold back their tears and withdraw from contact, sometimes for moments, sometimes forever. What if we could or would do as our young ones show us—express our feelings when we feel them and when finished, move spontaneously back into present focus?

To the extent that you learned as a child that: "Big boys (or girls) don't cry;" "Don't raise your voice;" "Stop crying, you're okay...," it may be difficult for you to make a shift into celebrating sobs as a form of healing. It also may be hard to allow your children to express their feelings openly without trying to stop the process.

You might remind yourself, "My child or partner is doing just what he needs to do. There's nothing here that needs fixing. The best thing that I can do is just be here and encourage the process until he or she is finished."

If you have been holding back tears for a lifetime, it can initially be overwhelming to begin to feel deeply. A lot of people are afraid that if they start crying they'll never stop. Hundreds of times we have said the same thing: "It's really common for those tears to feel scary, but I've never had a client who couldn't stop crying." But when first acknowledging old feelings that have been denied you may feel like a dam is breaking.

TROUBLESHOOTING: WHEN CRYING IS INEFFECTIVE

Several common roadblocks inhibit the potential healing effects of crying. One thing that can keep you from being able to feel better after crying is not accessing and fully expressing your feelings. To have a "good cry," stay with whatever you are feeling and try not to get distracted by thoughts. People often stop themselves from crying with thoughts like "The person that hurt me was just having a bad day (or life!)," or "I love my father—I can't be upset at him about such a little thing…" By calling a halt to this natural process of release, you miss out on the potential benefits of letting go. Put the positive thinking temporarily on hold. After a good cry, you'll often come to a spontaneous acceptance of the other person or upsetting situation. The process works best in this order, due to the manner in which our brains operate and the need to get our emotionality settled down. The adage is, "Handle the feelings first and *then* do your forgiving, thinking, and/or problem solving."

At the other extreme is crying for too long, getting lost or mired in negative emotions, or staying stuck in your story and being a victim. Our suggestions: take some breaths, shift into forgiving thoughts, wash your face, smell the roses, count your blessings, and finally think about what there is to learn so as to avoid repeating similar hurtful situations. The idea is to strike a balance between Pollyanna-like denial on one hand, and doom and gloom on the other. Ask yourself if you might be avoiding tears by underplaying how badly you feel or by repeatedly telling others how awful things are instead of having a good cry.

Crying can also be ineffective if focusing on the "wrong" thing. In other words, you may be upset about something other than what you think. Things can get confused like this because the emotional brain links upsets that are symbolically related and packages them together. If you are upset about how your boss treated you today, you are more likely to go home and burst into tears over something that wouldn't normally upset you. Cry first about what you think you are upset about, and then let your mind wander around to see if you are *also* upset about something else from the immediate or even distant past.

Some people have anger underneath their tears but are afraid to "go there." This pattern is common with those who have been socialized to think that anger is a bad thing. If that's the case, try to be more aware of and accepting of your anger and focus your attention in that direction. Feelings can also shift from anger to hurt, laughter to tears and then back again while you are expressing them. They just want to come out. Over time you can learn to just trust the process. Your body can relearn what you naturally knew as a young child and guide you toward what it needs to heal.

Finally, don't feel silly if there are times when you think you might need to cry but aren't sure why you are upset. Often in the middle of our tears, or even near the end of the release process we'll figure out why we're upset.

WHAT ABOUT ISSUES FROM OUR CHILDHOOD?

In every conceivable manner, the family is link to our past, bridge to our future.
-Alex Haley

Sometimes even under the best of conditions, people just aren't ready to express their feelings about old wounds. It can be too overwhelming, particularly for children who have experienced abuse or painful losses. Some wait until adulthood before they finally muster up the courage and strength to face their pain. If this is the case with you or a loved one, the place to start is just to notice what you are experiencing in your body, in your thoughts and with your feelings.

We all have "defense mechanisms" that are very much like the circuit breakers or fuses in your house. If you try to use your toaster, microwave, and iron on the same circuit, there's a good chance the system will overload and shut itself off. The same is true with human defenses. When things are overwhelming we shut down until we're more able to face what we need to in order to heal. This is part of the fight-flight-freeze response we described earlier. Often it's not until a crisis is over and we feel out of danger that we can safely express what we were feeling along the way.

HELPING OTHERS HEAL THROUGH PAIN

From our own personal experience as well as the reports of thousands of clients, crying with another person present seems to have a greater benefit than crying alone. Perhaps this is because we tend to stay with our feelings longer and deeper when another person is there to support us. This seems to be true for other feelings as well. Since many people have been shamed for their tears or watched others being teased about crying, a supportive family member may even need to encourage tearful expression rather than simply accepting it. When we are in our tears it can be all too easy to distract ourselves, feel embarrassed, or think of something else to do…like the laundry.

The role of a good listener is simply to be present (no talking!), offering mild encouragements now and then. "Go ahead, just let it out." "It's okay to cry." "That's good…" As hard as it might be, try to refrain from rubbing and patting. Physical movement can distract an upset person from their tears and the release process. Our physical movements can also be an expression of our own discomfort with another's crying. Sometimes what makes someone else's tears uncomfortable to us is the fact that we haven't dealt with our own.

A husband was talking about the possibility of being deported and his wife began to cry. He moved his chair over and held her arm tenderly, but then a few moments later started to massage her arm a little. She stopped crying. Despite his best intentions, he was inhibiting her

release. When he stopped patting her, she returned to some good sobs
that she'd long held in.

The way we speak about crying also helps to override the
social conditioning that has labeled it as something to hide or be
embarrassed about. We'll often ask clients, "When was the last
time you had a good cry?" Think about how you encourage or
discourage your own or family member's tears. Perhaps you might
even ask how you might best be of assistance when another needs
to cry. Does your child or partner cry best when they are held, or
not? Discovering your best supportive role is a treasure to share
with each other.

Due to old family "rules," teasing in school, etc., some people
are embarrassed by even the remote possibility of crying in front
of others. If you are facing this uphill climb, you might choose
to first relearn how to cry on your own. For example, if you are
mourning the loss of a loved one, you can deliberately activate your
feelings by looking at a picture of that person and speak to them,
saying things like "I love and miss you so much... I think about you
when... I remember the time when we... You sure made me mad
when... Why did you have to leave?"

TIPS & TOOLS FOR ANGER EXPRESSION

Anger is a signal, and one worth listening to.
-Harriet Lerner

When we are angry or upset it can be quite a challenge
to contain ourselves and to edit our words so we don't hurt our
relationship. But how do we stop our amygdalas from taking over
when we're trying to talk out our feelings with someone? Even
when expressed in a constructive fashion, anger can be difficult or
scary to share, both for the sender and the receiver. One good way
to improve the chances of positive communication with others is by
first expressing some of our anger on our own. If we can become
comfortable with and release some of our anger by ourselves, its
power can be reduced and *then* channeled into conversation and
constructive action.

Anger is like fire. It can destroy an entire village, but it can also be used for cooking. We want to be able to use anger in constructive ways to protect ourselves and speak up about our wants and needs, but without hurting others! Our clients have taught us a wide range of methods to vent anger in this manner, many of which have to do with moving major muscle groups in the body.

WAYS TO RELEASE ANGER ON YOUR OWN

Holding on to anger is like grasping a hot coal with the intent of throwing it at someone else; you are the one who gets burned.
-The Buddha

A precautionary note: The following methods are not advised for people with a history of violence or explosions of anger. These suggestions are intended to *prevent* any expression of verbal or physical aggression, and work best with those who are either out of touch with anger or scared of it. For people who have anger control difficulties, we recommend professional help and guidance before attempting the exercises below.

There are some excellent means of releasing anger on your own by thinking about what you are angry about while moving major muscle groups. Using safety, good judgment, and physical caution, the following are options for what we call "therapeutic exercise."

- Do some form of aerobic exercise and work up a sweat.
- Kneel next to your bed or a firm pad and pound with your fists in a chopping motion.
- Lie on your back and have a temper tantrum, kicking your legs and pounding with your arms at the same time.
- Use a punching bag or pound a tennis racket on a mattress.
- Safely throw rocks into the ocean or a lake.
- Rip a newspaper into tiny pieces.
- Stand and push against a wall.
- Find your own creative means of expression.

Here's a description of the process:

1. Focus your expression toward the "situation" you are upset about rather than directing it toward others.
2. Think of this method as a means of releasing your feelings in order to feel better, but without the intention of wishing anyone ill will. If you have spiritual inclinations, say a prayer or intention that this will enable you to shift into a benign acceptance of the upsetting circumstances.
3. Find a place where you can make a little noise without freaking out or bothering others. You can muffle sounds of vocalizing by placing a washcloth in your mouth and biting down.
4. Call to mind and visualize the events that made you mad.
5. Move your muscles and work up a sweat.
6. Think about the words you wanted to say but have been holding back. Avoid editing yourself and express the anger right from your gut. If you feel comfortable, even utter a few swear words.
7. Keep it up until you are exhausted and spent. Take some deep sighs and exhalations to blow out the remaining tension.
8. If you like, after you catch your breath again, focus on another feeling memory you want to let go of and repeat the process.

If you use these methods in conjunction with aerobic exercise, be sure to choose an activity that safely allows you to focus your attention on your upsets. It's *not* advised to do this releasing process while speeding on your bike at twenty miles per hour. Swimming is one of our personal favorites because it is safer and there is the added benefit of being able to scream out tension as you exhale into the water.

For people who are afraid of, or not in touch with, anger, these actions can feel embarrassing or fake for a short time, but it can be like starting a Model T. You have to crank it up at first, but it all begins to work when the feelings engine kicks into gear.

Naomi came to therapy upset about her husband's leaving her for a younger woman. Passive by nature, she'd put up with years of his being dominant in the relationship. She began to have difficulty sleeping at night and her children complained that they had become the brunt of her anger at their dad.

Most people have a terrible time getting enough sleep under circumstances like these. Their nervous systems are activated in the same way that a mother bear becomes vigilant and aggressive when her cubs are threatened. A lack of sleep further increases irritability.

Naomi found a way to scream and pound her anger out on a couch cushion, not once, but almost daily. She not only slept better after venting but, with a reduction of the tension, also felt more comfortable being assertive in the decisions she and her husband had to make about the kids. She learned to be less afraid of her anger.

The purpose of these methods, we repeat, is not to justify feeling wronged or act out your anger. You are not rehearsing it to blow off steam toward others in a hurtful way. You also don't want to stay stuck in a story that keeps you being a victim. Rather, you are empowering yourself by being open and honest, owning the truth of your feelings, and being responsible to "take your own garbage out." You are letting go of what keeps you from being more loving and accepting of others, even if they have hurt you. Additional means of softening angry feelings will be discussed in Chapter 8, Seeing the Positive.

As a final note, we have had remarkable success prescribing "therapeutic exercise" to clients struggling with feelings of fear as well. Using the same guidelines, simply work up to a level of aerobic exertion, think about what you are afraid of and yell in your mind at the fear, all at the same time.

EMOTIONS ARE CONTAGIOUS

Children are natural mimics: They act like their parents in spite of every attempt to teach them good manners.
-Anonymous

MIRROR NEURONS

An important discovery from the world of neuroscience and brain imaging is the existence of mirror neurons, first seen in monkeys and later found in humans (Iacoboni, 2008). Whenever we are observing someone else, our mirror neurons fire, mimicking in our brains what is going on in the brain of the other person. When we see emotions in another's face, we immediately sense that same feeling in ourselves. This discovery helps us to understand why children learn through imitating and how empathy is wired in biologically. Interestingly enough, the human brain prefers happy faces and recognizes them more quickly than negative facial expressions.

When it comes to families, mirror neurons have important implications. We are constantly impacting and being affected by the mood states of those around us. Haven't you had the experience of feeling perfectly fine and meeting up with your husband or wife who looks angry or upset only to have them ask you why you are upset with them? Now we know that a subtle unconscious dance is going on behind the scenes. Although misery may not love company, misery finds company quickly when the mirror neurons fire. Equally true, if you yawn or get the giggles, you are sure to be joined by people around you.

Tending to our own emotions, learning to center ourselves, and taking slow deep breaths are actually among the most powerful interventions that we can make with others in our presence. This is especially true for helping to calm your child or partner, particularly when they are going through a difficult moment. They will gradually climb into your own mood state. If not, the likely alternative is that you will both be bathing in a sea of painful feelings.

Research has also shown that the less powerful partner in a couple will more often make a shift to mimic the other's emotions (Anderson, C., et al., 2003.) Although we will discuss issues of power at more length in Chapter 5, the person who "has more power" tends to be the one who has more influence when it comes to making decisions about things like spending money, childrearing, or social plans. What this means is that one person in the room, particularly the one with more power, can unconsciously dictate the emotional temperature of a family in either a positive or negative direction.

In summary, learning to recognize and work with our emotions is an important undertaking not only for our individual health and happiness but also for the overall well-being of our relationships. This process is a lifelong practice. We use the word practice very consciously. Emotional management is a discipline, tended to moment by moment, practicing while never perfecting. We move through the ever-changing dance of pleasant and unpleasant, choreographed by the positive and negative emotions that are evoked just by being human. The journey to get in touch with and express feelings constructively can be a rocky road, but the net result is well worth the trip.

Now that you better understand the nature of this Key, you may want to go back and re-score yourself in the Current Family Assessment.

KEY #2 TIPS: EXPRESSING FEELINGS

- Be aware of and express feelings in a constructive way—not too much or too little.
- Maintain a 5:1 ratio of positive/ negative interactions.
- Remember that crying and constructive emotional expression can be a powerful means of healing.
- Take a break when emotions get high.
- Use exercise as a means of feelings release, particularly with fear and anger.
- Use calming methods such as centering and slow deep breaths.

CHAPTER THREE

KEY # 3
ADAPTING TO CHANGE

It is not the strongest of the species that survive,
nor the most intelligent, but the one most responsive to change.
-Charles Darwin

*C*hange may be the only constant in life. Changes bring loss and gain, opportunity and crisis, excitement and anxiety. Challenge accompanies every change, a characteristic that is not for the faint of heart. The ability to adapt is instrumental to the family's capacity to evolve new structure, patterns, and roles as inevitable changes occur. Some of the changes each family must respond to are the normal developmental changes that happen in the course of the life cycle from birth to death. More unpredictable are accidents, sudden disabilities, the effects of war, environmental change and economic instability.

More than ever, psychology and sociology scholars have been studying key processes that promote effective ways to adapt to change, handle stress, and manage life's formidable challenges. The last twenty years has seen a proliferation of books on "resilience." The definition of resilience, first employed to describe physical materials, is the ability to return to original form after being bent, compressed, or stretched out of shape. In psychological terms, it is the ability to recover quickly from disruptive change or misfortune without being overwhelmed or acting in a harmful way.

TWENTY-FIRST CENTURY FAMILIES

Progress always looks like destruction.
-John Steinbeck

Family structure evolves with every generation. Families in the new millennium face extraordinary challenges due to unprecedented changes in the norms and structures of societies around the world; they are being forced to adapt to change at an alarming and accelerated pace.

What used to be referred to as the nuclear family, a two-parent married heterosexual couple with a male breadwinner supported by a stay at home mom, is no longer the norm. This model has given way in our postmodern world to complex, extended households that are more fluid and far more susceptible to change than ever before.

Understanding the current social and economic trends in our culture is important for several reasons: first, because we have the tendency to compare ourselves, often negatively, to others; and second, because we can get overly judgmental when we don't have the facts. In our therapy practice, we are constantly asked about what is "normal." If normal is defined as what is currently the social norm or typical pattern, "normal" is for both parents to work outside the home during the time the children are being raised. Even so, many working moms are still plagued by guilt.

> *One of the times that I was self-critical was when I became a mother of two active boys. In my personal efforts to do everything right, I judged myself about not cooking homemade meals often enough, not getting enough sleep or exercise, or not spending enough quality time with my kids. My mom seemed to do it all and she had three kids! I didn't stop to factor in, until nudged by a dear friend, that I was simultaneously working full time, something my mom didn't have to do. –Debra*

There has been a steady decline in the rate of marriage in the United States as reported in *The State of Our Unions* (Wilcox, 2009.) This is due to a number of different factors. First, both men and women are getting married for the first time at older ages (averaging twenty-eight for men and twenty-six for women). More adults, both straight and gay, are choosing to cohabitate. The divorce rate still averages around fifty percent and the trend toward increasing numbers seems to have leveled off. Households undergo changes over time, shrinking as children leave the nest and expanding again as more young adults "boomerang" back into parental homes. Simultaneously our elderly citizens are living much longer, often returning to live with adult sons and daughters. Many have chronic health conditions and need special care and supervision.

The experience of children is also changing. According to the annual report, *America's Children: Key National Indicators of Well-Being* (2010), in 2008, forty-one percent of children were born to unmarried women; twenty-two percent of all children have at least one foreign-born parent; twenty-one percent of kids aged five to seventeen speak a language other than English at home; and nearly one in five live in poverty. The racial and ethnic diversity of America is undergoing a sea change and there is no end in sight.

In addition to changes in gender roles, changes in structures due to more working parents, and changes in family forms, there are enormous technological changes afoot. According to a Nielsen survey (2004), almost three quarters of American households have Internet access at home. Technology has brought many opportunities but with it many stresses for families. Through TV and the Internet, we've hatched an inescapable pop culture replete with images of sex, violence, materialism, games, and almost constant virtual connection. Is there anything that isn't changing?, we might ask.

DEVELOPING RESILIENCE

It's not whether you get knocked down. It's whether you get up again.
-Vincent Lombardi

One important part of cultivating resiliency is how we think about change. We have described some of the many changes and challenges to help you think of family life as a grand improvisation, a journey into a new world never before explored. If you can think of it in this way, you will be less judgmental of yourself and your family members as you face the stresses of everyday life. **The cornerstone of adaptability is embracing change rather than trying to avoid it.**

Robert Brooks and Sam Goldstein, authors of *Raising Resilient Children* (2002), talk about stress-hardy individuals possessing what they call a "resilient mindset." There appears to be a genetic component that inoculates some individuals better than others against the negative effects of stress. But regardless of genetics, parents can teach their children to be more resilient. Just as children are vaccinated to avoid physical disease, we can help by inoculating them for the challenges they will face throughout life.

Brooks and Goldstein assert that resilient children share the following characteristics:

1. They have adults who relate to them with unconditional love, support, and encouragement.
2. They have excellent problem-solving skills.
3. They demonstrate self-discipline.
4. They are optimistic and recognize their strengths.
5. They view mistakes as experiences to learn from.

Since children are more likely to develop a resilient mindset and confidence when they are aware of their strengths, parents must identify and reinforce their children's areas of competence. Rather than trying to "fix" our children, we should search for ways to build on their strengths.

DEVELOPMENTAL CHANGES IN FAMILIES

Life is like riding a bicycle, in order to keep your balance, you must keep moving.
-Albert Einstein

Parents that are adaptable also remain aware of what kind and amount of parenting is age appropriate for their children. They recognize that the parenting needs of an infant are very different than those of two-year-olds, which are in turn vastly different than the needs of a six-, ten-, thirteen-, or a sixteen-year-old. They also adapt to their child's gender, individual temperament, and even how they function at different times of the day. The job of parenting would be easier if children would just grow more responsible in a continuous path, day by day as they grow older. No such luck. What really happens is that kids can change from one moment to the next like the weather in New England. Teens, for example, can be acting quite mature and a few hours later seem like they are ten years younger. You wonder who took over their bodies. Good parenting requires the ability to quickly adapt to these shifts. We like to describe it as a "dance," where we take our children's lead as to what kind of parenting they need at any given time.

Many people, before they have children of their own, believe that kids' personalities are completely determined by learning and socialization. After having a second or third child in the same family with each child exposed to the same parenting practices, they'll often realize that kids can have very different temperaments. We are each unique—more or less shy, more or less active, and certainly more or less emotional.

At each stage of childhood development different demands are placed on the parents and other family members to give the child varying amounts of supervision, structure, and independence—versus complete freedom. Whenever any family member crosses the threshold of a new stage of development, there will undoubtedly be a need for new rules, roles, and ways of interacting. Families commonly go through a difficult period of increased turbulence whenever one of these new milestones is reached.

It is no coincidence that the most common times for families to seek counseling is at these developmental transitions—when the young couple has their first baby; the infant turns into a toddler; the young child enters school for the first time; the child becomes an adolescent; the young adult leaves home; the grandparents become ill and can't live alone anymore.

When one person in a family makes big changes, the whole family is shaken up. Sometimes another member becomes "symptomatic" and the whole family needs a course correction. Marriages are often strained when children leave home. The birth of a new baby, even when planned and anticipated with joy, brings grandparents back into the picture along with unresolved issues buried for years.

Sometimes change happens through unanticipated events like a job promotion and relocation, the sudden illness of a family member requiring more time and care, or the unplanned pregnancy of a teen. Symptomatic behavior in one family member can be an expression of the family's struggle with the enormity of the change.

A single parent mom was seeking advice about her three children. They had all been doing quite well until they began to fight constantly with one another. The mom had assumed that the bickering was related to their "growing older" until things got pretty bad. One of her sons put their parrot in the microwave and almost turned it on. The bird was okay but she decided the family needed help.

It didn't take long to figure out that the kids were upset about the family's plans to move. The mom had been accepted to graduate school and they were moving to another part of the state. She wanted to avoid her own pain, fearing that to feel at all would mean she'd fall apart and not be able to attend to all the things she needed to do. She had also been overeating and had gained a lot of weight. After becoming more comfortable expressing her own feelings, she was able to guide the kids in doing the same. As the kids faced and expressed their feelings about moving and saying goodbye to their friends, their conflict was dramatically reduced.

RITES OF PASSAGE

Only in growth, reform and change, paradoxically enough, is true security to be had.
-Anne Morrow Lindbergh

Rites of passage are an important aide to processes of adaptation in families. Cultures across the ages have celebrated the many developmental milestones that occur,—bar mitzvahs, graduation ceremonies, baby showers, and wakes. The following case example shows how a newly created ritual can be used to help things shift.

Gloria and Walter, a couple in their seventies, came for therapy because Walter was upset that his wife was treating him like a child. He didn't like the fact that she wouldn't let him write his own checks or have any credit cards. The back-story was that Walter was an alcoholic who had been irresponsible with money for thirty years, but was now seven years sober. He wanted another chance to prove himself instead of being seen in the old, negative light. In addition to Walter's successful sobriety, the couple shared that their forty-five-year-old son had finally left home in the past month.

At the end of our first session, it was suggested that the couple create a ritual together to symbolize the changes they had made. They needed to celebrate Gloria's success at mothering both her children and her husband for so many years. She had done a fabulous job of carrying the lion's share of responsibility and caretaking. The new marriage contract would value Walter as an equal partner.

Walter bought her flowers and they had a dinner celebration acknowledging her accomplishment while symbolizing that her job was now complete. Surprisingly, they called to cancel their second session, insisting that everything had changed between them and they no longer needed help. Follow-up phone calls years later confirmed that a lasting change had taken place after their ritual.

GOOD GRIEF!

Without your wounds where would your power be? The very angels themselves cannot persuade the wretched and blundering children on earth as can one human being broken in the wheels of living. In love's service, only the wounded soldiers can serve.
-Thornton Wilder

As can be seen from these examples, many families struggle because they are unable to deal appropriately with change or loss. Loss is inevitable—illness, disappointments, growing up, growing old—all are part of life. How a person copes with loss is a learned process, and we can incorporate healthy strategies or ineffective ones. Examples of ineffective strategies include the actions of those who go through a divorce or the death of a loved one and cannot really get on with life, becoming stuck and living in the past rather than fully experiencing their grief through mourning.

Healthy grieving requires full awareness and expression of feelings of anger and sadness over a period of time, sometimes weeks or months or even years for a severe loss. The appropriate expression of feelings being allowed and even encouraged (as described in the last chapter) is a big part of how we get through painful transitions. Subsequent to this healing process one naturally becomes capable of involvement in new relationships again. Different family members should be allowed to go through losses their own unique way—some expressing more sadness, others more angers—some quickly, others more slowly.

Do you remember how the emotional brain can keep us stuck in the past? When we have the ability to feel our feelings and release them, we can clean the slate. Feeling clear, being able to make decisions, having an open heart and being forgiving... these are the elements of our natural state that are all too often clouded by negative feelings. Once negativity is cleared, we can to move to a better place emotionally. This principle is just as true for mourning the loss of the family dog before getting a new one, as it is for grieving over a deceased spouse or the end of a marriage. The obvious difference is simply the amount of grief, and the amount of time necessary for the process to complete its course.

Another unfortunate pattern develops when people reach the sunset of their lives and begin to isolate themselves socially. Not letting themselves feel any longer, they will shut down their ability to let go of yet another friend who has passed away. Now we know that being older doesn't mean that we have to shut down due to these inevitable losses. Having lots of "good cries" and good support can make a world of difference.

The issue of adaptability brings up one of my favorite stories about my mother—one I often share with clients. Here's the setup. A female client, perhaps thirty or thirty-five years old, is seeking help for the loss of a relationship. She's convinced she'll never find another partner because she is over the hill and too old, and all the good men are taken. After empathizing with the real and very painful part of her loss, I'll eventually chime in, "But wait 'til I tell you about my mother!"

My mother was married three different times—first to my dad, and then to two other men, both of whom died while married to her. Her third husband died when she was eighty years old. She sent out her annual Christmas letter describing her loss, and an old friend, Erasmus, responded. He called her on the phone, came to town, they soon "tied the knot" and the rest is history...

My mom is now eighty-eight, Erasmus is ninety-one, and by all accounts she has found her perfect soulmate... the man of her dreams... the love of her life. They've been together for eight years, and she has never been so happy and even giddy in love.

If we compare my mom to most people her age, there is a distinct attribute that helps explain why she, unlike many, has been able to thrive in a new relationship in her eighties. She knows how to grieve, cry, and get angry in constructive ways. Letting go of feelings allowed her let go of the past and open to a new relationship. —Don

OTHER TIPS AND TOOLS

Being able to grieve isn't only about the ability to express emotions when necessary. It involves other dimensions as well. One is found in a resilient mindset, and another in understanding loss from a broader spiritual, religious, or philosophical perspective. We will discuss the importance of this dimension more fully in Chapter 8. But suffice it to say, if we have learned that bad things can happen to good people and that suffering is an inevitable part of life, we are less likely to take our losses quite so personally or to think that we are alone in our suffering. When such situations arise, we see them as challenges to learn from rather than as stress to avoid.

An important aspect of considering change that you are facing is to determine which part, if any, is something over which you have control. Millions of people have found "The Serenity Prayer" taught in AA and Al-Anon to be a useful touchstone or reminder of a resilient mindset:

God grant me the serenity to accept the things I cannot change, the courage to change the things I can, and the wisdom to know the difference.
-Reinhold Niebuhr

There are tools and aids that can help families cope with change and crisis, and there are many excellent books and resources on resiliency in our section on Self-Help Resources.

THE VALUE OF SOCIAL SUPPORT

Another important component of being able to grieve is taking comfort from others. After decades of research, we know that there is a significant correlation between supportive relationships and both physical and psychological health. Controlling for risk factors such as smoking, drinking, exercise, and obesity, Berkman and Syme (1979) found that socially isolated individuals tend to die younger than those who are more connected. Social support is a powerful medicine for surviving life's losses. When the family sees loss as an inevitable part of life and that their role is simply to be there for one another, they can find hope and solace together. If, on the other hand, family members define a given event as insurmountable, they are less able to cope.

A resilient family member remains open to receiving help rather than closing down. Social support can come from family members, but also friends, church members, volunteers, Big Sisters, almost anyone who can provide empathy, love, and contact. Other forms of social support include receiving concrete help like meals, money, or running errands in times of need. A support system can also provide us with useful information, encouragement, and hope. It is little wonder that in survey after survey, most men and women describe their family or their intimate partner or friendships as their most valued asset.

If you are able to cry on someone's shoulder, you can receive the added benefit of both comfort and social support. Research by William Frey (1985) found that eighty-five percent of women and seventy-three percent of men reported feeling better after crying. In spite of how much relief can come from crying, lots of men still feel bound by cultural expectations to be strong and stoic. When men are able to cry, they most often do so with a trusted female or alone.

There are times in all of our lives when we can't seem to figure out what we are doing wrong or how to see things differently in order to move forward. Sharing our grief with others also gives us a new perspective. We usually get encouragement or prodding or empathy. Just taking the step of asking for help can help move us from the stance of hopeless and helpless to the beginning of empowerment.

People who take action, even the smallest movement, in the face of crisis will weather difficulties better than those who remain shut down and shut off from others. Finally, one of the best ways to teach our children self-care is by seeking help for ourselves when needed. When we fly in airplanes, we are instructed to first put the oxygen mask on our own face, and then on our children. Remember those mirror neurons? Our children depend on us to take the lead so that they can follow, especially in times of change.

SELF-CARE ROUTINES

Life is a succession of lessons which must be lived to be understood.
-Ralph Waldo Emerson

Learning and practicing self-care is yet another way that we remain healthy and adaptable. Given the demands of the world, especially now with most families having both parents working, we are seeing the results of a rapid decline in self-care.

Our lives are out of balance. We aren't getting enough exercise, healthy food, or sleep. We are facing an epidemic of childhood obesity in America. Thirty-seven percent of kids are overweight. According to a report on children and media by Rideout, et al. (2010), eight to eighteen-year-olds spend an average of more than seven-and-a-half hours a day in front of a television, computer, and/or handheld screen. Our kids are constantly bombarded with stimuli, often unable to quell their boredom in the old-fashioned ways like going outside to play.

If we are, in the "good" times, stressed out, teetering on the edge of health problems, and struggling to get everything done, what happens when change hits the family? It is far more likely to precipitate a crisis if we have not created some prior structures to handle what should be the givens: meals, bedtime routines, homework, chores, regular exercise, and date nights for couples. Some of these issues go far beyond the scope of this book but are important to mention. Others have become frequent points of discussion in our work, and we'd like to address them here.

SLEEP

Recent studies (Colten and Altevogt, 2006) estimate that fifty to seventy million Americans are chronically sleep deprived. The long-term effects of sleep loss have been associated with numerous health risks including hypertension, diabetes, obesity, depression, heart attack, and stroke. These statistics are worse than even a few years ago.

Children (roughly aged five to twelve) who are no longer napping but haven't yet reached puberty are particularly vulnerable to sleep deprivation. This is because they can't "sleep in" like teens and adults. Teenagers, for example, have the ability to stay up until midnight during weekdays and sleep until two in the afternoon on the weekends. But younger children can't do this. We have never found an exception. A young child who has stayed up until midnight is rarely capable of sleeping past eight in the morning.

Pediatricians are a frequent source of referrals for our clinic. They send us young kids demonstrating emotional outbursts, acts of aggression, irritability, and/or attention deficit challenges. How does this relate to sleep? We now know that the most important time when we replenish serotonin in our brains is during sleep. This neurotransmitter is essential to learning, staying calm, and feeling good, and is produced almost exclusively during REM sleep, while we are dreaming. Not enough sleep and you've got an irritable child subject to meltdown.

The diagnosis and the cure are both simple. *If you have to wake your young child up in the morning, they aren't getting enough sleep!* Try putting them to bed fifteen minutes earlier for a few days, and see if they wake up by themselves. If they still aren't waking up by themselves by the time they need to be up, shift their bedtime earlier by another fifteen minutes, etc. You might be surprised how many problems either disappear or become controllable by adjusting this one daily routine.

EXERCISE

Exercise and application produce order in our affairs, health of body, cheerfulness of mind, and these make us precious to our friends.
–Thomas Jefferson

According to the Center for Disease Control (Lee, et al., 2006) only 3.8 percent of elementary schools, 7.9 percent of middle schools and 2.1 percent of high schools provide daily physical education or its equivalent for the entire school year. Twenty-two percent of schools do not require students to take any physical education at all, despite the fact that research has demonstrated some amazing benefits of regular aerobic exercise. Most of us are familiar with the contribution exercise makes to helping our hearts, physical health, and the ability to keep our weight in check, etc. We also know that exercise helps to reduce tension and stress while boosting endorphins and good feelings. It has also been shown to lower anxiety, alleviate depression, and prevent numerous medical problems.

Now we know that regular exercise is also helpful to our brains, which is how physical activity ties into the issue of adaptability. John Ratey, M.D., in *Spark: The Revolutionary New Science of Medicine and the Brain* (2008), has been instrumental in compiling research about and advocating exercise for children and adults. His work is based upon hundreds of studies.

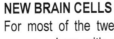

NEW BRAIN CELLS

For most of the twentieth century, scientists assumed that we were born with all of the neurons (brain cells) that we would ever get, and that our brains were fully hardwired by adolescence. A Swedish researcher (Eriksson, 1998) was the first to discover that we grow new neurons throughout life. Now we also know that exercise is a powerful way to increase the number of new neurons that we can generate. Studies have shown that rats receiving exercise produce at least three times as many new brain cells on a daily basis as non-exercising rats (Ratey, 2008).

Through the release of certain proteins, exercise contributes to learning skills and heightens our senses. It improves motivation, confidence and even our tendency to establish and maintain social connections.

It also improves our ability to be kind to others because it strengthens the connections in the prefrontal cortex that calm the amygdala (and therefore our emotional outbursts). Schools where aerobic exercise has been integrated into the curriculum have shown dramatic decreases in acts of aggression. Exercise has also been shown to block addictive cravings of all sorts. Finally, it helps both kids and adults to focus and maintain attention better, and even those who are challenged with Attention Deficit Disorder (ADD or ADHD).

If exercise were a medication, given that it is free, people would be lined up for blocks to get some. Unfortunately, because it takes time and commitment in a world where families are massively overcommitted, this simple solution to many ills is often left by the wayside. Given that schools haven't quite gotten their act together on the exercise front, what better way to spend time together as a family than to get outside and move around a lot?

We have only touched upon some of the typical changes that happen over the course of the family life cycle. There are countless other subtle and not-so-subtle changes that each person must face with the passage of time. Learning to let go and go with the flow rather than resist the tides of change distinguishes happier families.

Now that you better understand the nature of this Key, you may want to go back and re-score yourself in the Current Family Assessment.

KEY #3 TIPS: ADAPTING TO CHANGE

■ Recognize and encourage others' unique strengths.

■ Treat mistakes as helpful learning opportunities.

■ Practice habits of regular sleep, exercise and self-care.

■ Rather than trying to "fix" your child or partner, search for ways to build on their strengths.

■ Identify and adapt to your child's temperament, age, and gender.

■ Find social support from family, friends, social and volunteer groups, faith groups, etc.

CHAPTER FOUR

KEY # 4
SHARING TIME TOGETHER

The family. We were a strange little band of characters trudging through life sharing diseases and toothpaste, coveting one another's desserts, hiding shampoo, borrowing money, locking each other out of our rooms, inflicting pain and kissing to heal it in the same instant, loving, laughing, defending, and trying to figure out the common thread that bound us all together.
-Erma Bombeck

*W*hat makes "families" so important? Why do some people feel so connected, while others say they don't feel like a family? How is a family supposed to feel? And how can you create this precious feeling?

Although families have changed in form, they have not declined in their importance. Although most adults agree that children benefit from knowing their relatives and family history, the reasons for valuing family connections are varied. In the past and in many parts of the world, family bonds were necessary to ensure survival. We turned to extended family for economic support, for help with childrearing, for caring for sick or elderly members or simply for emotional connection. Not only is our capacity to bond hardwired in our brains, the importance of duty to family has been written about and discussed for thousands of years.

The wish to seek a deep sense of family connection and commitment is universal. All of the major models of family systems theory include this crucial component. **In healthy families there is a sense of cohesion or family togetherness brought about by sharing positive, life-affirming experiences.** Our families give us a sense of identity, reminding us of who we are and what is unique about us. They are also the context, the background, out of which our individuality grows.

Much of this sense of family identity is passed down through names, which is why the naming of children and the taking on of maternal or paternal last names is so culturally important. Shakespeare's tragedy of *Romeo and Juliet* is as brilliant today as when it was written because it is the story of the clash between familial loyalty and romantic love. "Blood is thicker than water" goes the familiar proverb meant to explain how there is a particular kind of loyalty that is observed not only within nuclear families but with extended family as well.

What gives some families a stronger sense of connection? The answer is quite simple. We must spend time together, or if separated by geography, spend time communicating. Only by making the time to share the details of our daily lives as well as our successes, hardships, and future dreams can we reap the rewards of our familial bonds. Although quality is more important, quantity is also essential. Twenty-first century families are simply hungry for more quality contact with mom, dad, sibs, and grandparents. We hear constant complaints from clients about spending too much time at work and barely seeing their spouses, let alone having enough quality time with them.

Just as we learned the importance of social support from outside the family, we know that people who cultivate extended family relationships are at an advantage emotionally and are often more successful in their personal lives. Both children and adults benefit from these relationships during times of great stress, such as tragedy, death, or divorce. They also reap the rewards when joyous events enter their lives, whether it is a new job, a new child, or a milestone birthday. As medical science steadily extends the average lifespan, children today are fortunate to have more opportunities for interaction with extended family members.

THE IMPORTANCE OF RITUALS AND ROUTINES

I remember my mother's prayers and they have followed me. They have clung to me all my life.
-Abraham Lincoln

Most of us remember certain time-honored traditions from our past...the story read to us every night before going to bed, the special weekly meal at our grandparents house, holiday times and decorations, cookouts in the summer. What makes these simple actions so memorable?

Family rituals can include religious observances, such as attending services together, saying daily prayers or nonreligious celebrations such as holiday or birthday celebrations, giving and granting of nicknames, traditional games or songs. Family routines are daily or weekly interaction patterns like dinnertime, bedtime stories, assigned chores, or bath times.

Family rituals and routines are special ways of doing things that we repeat over and over again. In the same way that muscles grows stronger when you use them over and over again, so too sharing repeated experiences strengthens the family, giving it stability, order, and a feeling of belonging. Values and beliefs are often communicated through our traditions. Through repetition, we reinforce the unspoken message that family is important.

A review of thirty-two studies (Fiese, et al., 2002) affirmed that family routines (such as bedtime, chores, and dinnertime) and family rituals (such as birthdays, holiday celebrations, and family reunions) are associated with marital satisfaction, children's health, academic achievement, adolescents' sense of personal identity, and stronger family relationships. One study in the review found that children who had regular bedtime routines got to sleep sooner and woke up less frequently during the night than those with less regular routines. Regular routines in the household have even been found to shorten bouts of respiratory infections in infants.

Many families have abandoned routines as family members have conflicting demands on their time. The shared mealtime, once a hallmark of family time, has become less and less common. Can the lack of rituals create problems? It seems that no specific routine is crucial, but the presence of routines and rituals in general is beneficial and seems to serve a protective function.

Routines and rituals may also be especially important following a divorce, mitigating some of the negative effects. Routines and rituals provide consistency when the structure of the family itself is threatened. One study showed that families able to preserve their rituals despite parental alcoholism, were less likely to transmit alcoholism to their offspring (Bennett, Wolin, & Reiss, 1988). We also know that routines foster better adjustment in families when one member is severely ill or has chronic pain.

The positive effects of this kind of consistent connection are numerous and profound. The research (Eisenberg, et al., 2004) also indicates that children from families who have meaningful family rituals report fewer symptoms of anxiety, including both emotional worries and physical symptoms. At times of increased stress, family rituals and daily routines may offer one avenue for families to stabilize their lives and provide a sense of comfort. Or perhaps families who are able to create meaningful rituals in the first place are better equipped to respond to multiple stressors.

Most families have traditions and rituals around meaningful holidays. One of the many reasons these times can cause extra stress for families is when a couple has been unable to create their *own* rituals for celebration. This can be further complicated by religious or cultural differences.

Celia and Rick had been married for five years when they sought counseling. Their unfortunate annual "ritual" was to fight miserably between Thanksgiving and New Years'. They had dutifully spent each Thanksgiving with her family and Christmas with his parents and adult siblings. It wasn't much fun for either of them because they felt torn between pleasing their parents, themselves, and each other.

They realized that they had been inadvertently reinforcing each other's need to be "perfect" in the eyes of their parents and then took their resentments out on each other. They worked out some rituals for the holidays that were a reflection of their past traditions but with some new personal elements. The following year they reported having Christmas in their own home, Boxing Day festivities with both their extended families, and received the best present of all...no fighting.

TIPS & TOOLS FOR DEVELOPING ROUTINES

What greater thing is there for human souls than to feel that they are joined for life—to be with each other in silent unspeakable memories.
-George Eliot

Perhaps as you are reading this, you realize that your family would benefit from more deliberate routines. Two dimensions seem to be important: the degree to which routines are an integral part of family practices and the degree to which these activities have meaning for family members. In order for a routine to work, it must happen on a regular basis, someone must be responsible to plan and carry it out, and rules must be communicated to family members about their participation. Usually if one person (often the more motivated) takes leadership, the others will gladly follow.

Although at the beginning, it takes time, commitment, and repetition to get a new routine going, it almost always ends up saving time in the end. We are amazed at how many times we get the same reply when asking parents if they have the kids help with things like preparing meals, doing yard work, or feeding pets. They say, "It's easier and faster to do it myself" or "It's not worth all the complaining and sour faces so I just do it myself." When a routine is successfully instituted, everyone benefits. Children learn how to participate, the value of commitment is strengthened, and moms and dads eventually get a little extra time. For those of you who are skeptical about accomplishing this, we'll address more about parents taking charge in the next chapter.

Here are some examples of routines that we think work well. Universally, parents feel the most stress in the morning when trying to get the kids off to school and themselves to work, and in the evening seeing that homework is done, dinner eaten, baths or showers, and bedtime accomplished. More arguments and upset happen at these times. Establishing daily routines takes some of the stress away. Among the tools for family routines are star charts or check-off lists that give positive rewards for "mission accomplished." Many younger children jump at the chance of having morning or evening "games." Set the timer and have them compete to get their list done in faster and faster times. If you enforce bedtimes consistently, kids argue less about them. The same can be said for chores, homework, or bath time.

THE IMPORTANCE OF FAMILY MEALTIME

There are many positive benefits of having family dinners (or breakfasts) as often as your particular lifestyle allows. Aim for at least three or four times a week but don't abandon them all together if you can only do one or two. Start when the children are small, even though those mealtimes might be short. It will become the norm.

Besides providing a sense of family, eating together has other perks. Young children tend to eat healthier foods and to develop better eating habits from the start. Teens are less likely to retreat into their rooms. With more regular parent-child communication, problems surface more readily instead of remaining hidden. Mealtimes provide a time and place for in-depth talks, relaxation and catching up on family news.

TIPS & TOOLS FOR MEALTIME

1. First of all, make it a priority to share meals. Every family member should make the commitment that this time is sacred. Set a beginning and ending time and devote the meal to talking and having fun as a family. Turn off the television and, if necessary, record programs that can be watched after mealtime. Agree to take a break from phones and texting. There shouldn't be any reading unless what is being read is shared with everyone.
2. Be flexible about when, where, and what. Shared meals can come from the freezer or from a restaurant and can be simple and easy. If one parent or child can't make it until later in the evening, snack first so that you can eat when everyone is home. If you can't eat together every evening, start with some evenings. If dinners can't be arranged, try mornings. If weekdays are impossible, try weekends.
3. Create family traditions such as a family picnic night where simple meals can be eaten outside or in a nearby park. Trade off who gets to decide what the main course is so everyone gets a

voice. Make dinners special by lighting a candle or using special napkins. Have an occasional dinner in front of a TV show that everyone likes.

4. Let the kids be involved in ways that are appropriate to their age. Young children love to help and are more likely to enjoy the experience if engaged. Older kids take pride in making a simple dish or a complete meal for the family. In this way, they learn a bit about cooking and preparing at the same time.

5. In order to encourage conversation, give everyone a turn talking. Don't get into "adult only" conversations that are boring for the kids. Find topics that interest others and ask questions of each other. You are modeling table manners, social skills, and good eating habits in one fell swoop.

6. Try to keep nagging or discipline to a minimum so that mealtime can be fun. You can have rewards for participation or not arguing at the table. For example, a cooperating child could be released from dish duty.

FINDING JOY AND COMFORT

In family life, love is the oil that eases friction, the cement that binds closer together, and the music that brings harmony.
-Eva Burrows

Remember the old adage, "The family that plays together stays together."? Have fun as a family. There are lots of ways to play; it can be as simple as showing warmth, using tender names for one another, or appreciating each other's strengths, gifts, or contributions. It can be done through all forms of play. Many adults learn to play again after they have kids. Almost anything can be a game with babies and young children. Learn to have fun doing frivolous things and have fun doing work together. Exposing kids to a variety of activities keeps them learning and growing.

Healthy families find joy just being together. They care about one another's well-being and want each other to be happy. They comfort one another through the difficult times because they remember the good times. An important part of our sense of family cohesion is the fact that we have a shared history and the belief in a shared future. Through communication and through shared expression of feelings, we learn about each other's dreams and triumphs as well as each other's fears and worries.

One of our favorite things to do as a family is playing games. No surprise. I grew up as the youngest in a game-playing family. My father and older brothers taught me how to play craps and poker by the time I was six years old, much to my mother's chagrin. (They also taught me how to throw a football like a boy). On Don's side, he was constantly longing for someone to play games with as a boy. Once he punched his older sister in the stomach when she wouldn't play a game with him. After his mom fined him a quarter, it stopped the punching but not his desire for games.

As a couple we indulge in rousing sprees of Scrabble, card games, board games, Ping Pong, and charades, and spilled these passions to our kids. Now in their twenties, our boys still love to come home and play with us—proof that traditions live on. —Debra

FAMILY TIME ALTERNATIVES

In addition to spending time all together as a family, parents should create occasions where each parent has alone time with each child. Certain patterns or alliances are predictable. For example, it is natural for the firstborn to grow more connected to dad when a newborn comes onto the scene and is breastfeeding and therefore literally connected to mom. Ideally, however, alliances don't become rigid so that family "teams" persists over long periods of time. Variations of twosomes, for example, tend to work great. Each family member gets to have special alone time with every other member.

CREATE YOUR OWN RITUALS

Perhaps few of the traditions from your past hold meaning for you anymore. Or perhaps you have joined with a partner who comes from a very different cultural or religious background than you. There is no rule that says that you can't create your own new rituals. Many find this process very rewarding. Just as we can institute routines to help bring order out of the chaos, we can create rituals that have personal meaning for our family.

In order to do this, first think about what you intend to accomplish. Many couples choose to write their own wedding vows because the traditional ones don't communicate their current values. As they craft their intentions, they discover fundamental truths that they want to remember and hold as sacred.

The same practice can be applied when it comes to deciding on how your family is going to celebrate birthdays and holidays, as well as losses and death. What ritual do you use when you bury the dead hamster? Is there a way to acknowledge your daughter getting her period for the first time? What rituals of hello and goodbye do you have when greeting and leaving each other? If you don't know the answer, you may wish to reflect more on this Key.

The elements of this Key are the glue that holds families together. When anyone speaks of longing to "go home," (even a nonhuman like ET), we instantly know what they are feeling in their heart. Home is where the heart is, and what touch our hearts are expressions of love, caring, and commitment. The bond of love is cemented through time spent deliberately with one another, and through routines and rituals that are special to your family.

Now that you better understand the nature of this Key, you may want to go back and re-score yourself in the Current Family Assessment.

KEY #4 TIPS: SHARING TIME TOGETHER

- Enjoy time together playing and having fun.
- Create new rituals that are special to your family and you can do on a regular basis.
- Eat meals together more than once a week.

- Have established routines for bedtime, meals, and family time.
- Create opportunities to be with extended family at holidays or other occasions.
- Encourage each family member to take special alone time with every other member.

CHAPTER FIVE

KEY # 5
WHO'S IN CHARGE?

There is little less trouble in governing
a family than a whole kingdom.
-Montaigne

*G*uidebooks for new parents have been published almost every year since the 1930s, the most famous being Dr. Spock's, *Baby and Child Care* (1946). Research since that time has helped us to understand the parenting practices that foster competence, independence, and maturity in children and teens.

Family researchers have known for years that healthy families create environments that balance large doses of love and warmth with sufficient firmness and structure. Kids thrive in these settings. Without love and warmth they tend to feel abandoned and resentful, and without firmness and structure they will often become anxious and/or have behavior problems.

Not everyone parents in the same way. As we know from the first two Keys, families vary in how they communicate and express feelings. They also vary in amounts and forms of discipline and rules, and in levels of closeness and affection. Putting all of these factors together, psychologist Diana Baumrind (1967) described three different parenting styles: *authoritarian, authoritative,* and *indulgent.* Maccoby and Martin (1983) added a fourth style, *neglectful.* Research is under way to further explore these styles and their effectiveness within different ethnic groups and with different problematic behaviors in kids.

Authoritarian parents have a strict no-nonsense style. They do not negotiate or provide reasons for their requests. Children are expected to do it now "Because I said so." Debra's father, a former officer in the Marine Corps and a WWII vet, used to say, in classic authoritarian style, "When I say jump, I expect you to say 'How high?'" Authoritarian parents have high expectations and make lots of demands. They run a tight ship, expecting complete and immediate compliance. They are less responsive and tend to withhold praise and rewards. These parents expect children to act in a mature fashion at a fairly young age.

By contrast, parents who use a *permissive* or *indulgent* style are far more lenient with their kids. They exhibit lots of caring but exercise little control over children's behaviors. Permissive parents more often allow children to do what they want, relinquishing decisions to children (even fairly young ones) about when to go to bed, what they eat, what chores to do (if they even have any at all). Children in such families are often impulsive, demanding, and dependent on parents. Permissive parents demand little but still shower the children with warmth and affection. Given this combination, kids in this type of family often expect to get a lot and have their way.

Another style of parenting is *uninvolved* or *neglectful*. These parents are not only permissive but also indifferent to their children. Uninvolved parents both fail to set limits and make few demands on their children. Although they usually provide basic needs for food, shelter, and money, they show little warmth or caring. The children get the message that their parents' personal lives are more important than their parental duties.

Finally, there are the parents who use an *authoritative* style, balancing emotional support with clear boundaries and structure. Unlike their authoritarian counterparts who score high on demands and low on responsiveness to the children, or the permissive who score the opposite (high on responsiveness, low on demands), or the neglectful (low on both counts), authoritative parents score high on both dimensions. They encourage age-appropriate behavior from their children, but also provide rules and structure in a warm manner that incorporates give and take, explanations for why rules should be followed, and respect for their children's point of view and input. This style clearly incorporates the elements of the first four Keys, encouraging the child's voice and strengths while at the same time establishing expectations for cooperation and conformity to rules.

What does all this look like in practical terms? Consider the following parenting example:

Stephen and Paula, very caring and involved parents, brought their five-year-old son, Charlie, in for help with his behavior problems. Charlie was on the brink of being kicked out of his preschool because of defiant and aggressive behavior. His parents were desperate because their "little angel" had bitten the teacher's aide.

Charlie was about as cute as they come, but pranced around the office with the same "air" that had been described at school. At our first session, his mother handled his breaking of crayons and hanging out the window by saying in a sweet and tentative voice, "Now, Charlie, please don't do that, okay?" His dad didn't say anything until his son's behavior careened out of control, at which point he barked frightening orders. Paula criticized him for being too harsh on their little boy.

During the course of therapy, Stephen and Paula began to understand how experiences with their own parents had left scars that made it difficult to set limits with their son. Stephen recalled harsh treatment by his parents, and in a moving session expressed a lot of anger at his dad for having spanked him so much. Stephen's fear of his own pent-up anger spilling out on Charlie had rendered him incapable of being firm.

Paula, on the other hand, realized that she was copying her parents' lackadaisical style by giving Charlie too much freedom. The youngest of seven children, she had been all but ignored by her parents, who worked long hours and had little time for the children. In therapy, Paula grieved about the lack of parenting she received and her unfulfilled desire for nurturing. Little by little, she became better able to set appropriate limits for Charlie.

Stephen and Paula, like so many parents, needed education and coaching to become more authoritative. Stephen's background with an authoritarian father tilted him in the opposite direction, being too permissive. Paula's neglectful or at least permissive parents failed to model appropriate limit setting. Since neither of them had received love and effective limits, this couple was woefully unprepared for the normal challenges of a bright inquisitive child. They are not alone.

Countless parents are grappling with a child or adolescent who is "acting out" or exhibiting other problematic behavior that is often simply a cry for a more balanced form of discipline. For Stephen and Paula, the solution was two-tiered. They needed to provide consistent limits and they needed to learn to work together as a team. These are two essential elements set for creating a happy, healthy family.

FAMILIES THAT ARE TOO SOFT

How times have changed; a century ago minding one's children didn't mean obeying them.

-Anonymous

Over the past fifty years families of all socioeconomic and ethnic backgrounds have become significantly more soft or permissive than in the past (Penn and Zalesne, 2007). In part this shift is seen as a reaction to the overly stern or authoritarian parenting dealt out by previous generations, as is reflected in the often-uttered statement, "I'll never treat *my* kids the way I was brought up!" Other permissive parents grew up in families where their own parents were also too permissive.

One explanation links increased permissiveness to economic stress. As both mothers and fathers spend extra hours working outside the home, they have less time to be with their kids. The guilt stemming from this shortage of family time, and from divorce as well, often prompts parents to be more lenient—an understandable but unhelpful means of compensating. Although being together as a family is important, the quantity of time devoted to it is not nearly as crucial as the quality of interactions and the methods of discipline we use. In most families where kids are misbehaving, the hierarchy is upside down with the kids wielding more power than their parents.

> Sometimes children's fears and the reality of having too much power in a family are buried, but it's not uncommon for the feelings to be closer to the surface. Sara, a precocious four-year-old, and her parents arrived at the Institute for their first session. A teacher at Sara's preschool suggested they get some help for Sara's emotional outbursts and difficulties getting along with the other children. Midway through the session when Sara was asked who was the boss in her family, she pointed tentatively toward her dad. Her mom, in a fit of laughter, exclaimed, "That's so not true." Sara proudly blurted out, "I'm the boss! Mommy wants to be the boss, but I'm the boss. That's why we're here!"

When asked why they allow their children to wield so much power over them, many parents say that discipline might injure their child's self-esteem. In reality, letting children get away with too much can be as damaging to their feelings of self-worth as being too strict. When kids have too much power, they become anxious about the impulses they cannot control, and as a result they feel bad about themselves.

Another pattern of permissiveness develops when parents feel sorry for a child and proceed to allow inappropriate behavior. One mom realized in therapy that she had relaxed the rules too much with her eight-year-old daughter because of recent family traumas. The parents' divorce was immediately followed by the loss of their home in a wildfire. The child had lots of feelings about losing her family and all of her possessions, but was also acting out as a way of testing the boundaries. Receiving more limits and structure dramatically helped to lessen her anxieties.

Permissiveness can also come from a parent's fear of making waves or being in conflict with their children. It is too important for these parents to be their child's friend. The solution is often to help these parents find social support and more of a "life" outside of the family. This can help them to feel that they don't have all of their emotional eggs in one basket. We have a favorite adage about this dilemma:

> **If your child isn't upset with you at times, you probably aren't parenting very well.**

Although parents should be in charge, this doesn't mean that *they* deserve respect but their children don't. Respect should flow in both directions. Children who feel respected and understood for their feelings, in turn, listen better to their parents— not like little robots or bushy-tailed people pleasers, but also not like defiant insurrectionists. No child can be expected to do exactly what mom or dad says the very first time every time they say something. Children are still children, and it is part of their nature to stretch limits, test, and experiment with the world around them. However, parents who are loving and in charge know that they can enforce their requests, and when they "really mean it," their child will comply.

FAMILIES THAT ARE TOO STRICT

With a sweet tongue and kindness, you can drag an elephant by a hair.
-Persian proverb

At the other end of the power continuum are families that are too strict. Excessive control often stifles a child's spirit and leads to resentment and rebellion, as it did with seventeen-year-old Priscilla.

Priscilla, a bright student, had been "busted" in school for possession of marijuana. To be admitted back to classes, the school dictated that she and her parents had to undergo at least three family therapy sessions. Her parents, initially startled at the request to be involved in these sessions, soon recognized that they could be helpful agents of change.

In the first meeting we learned that the marijuana incident was only part of the story. Pricilla had also recently been doing poorly in classes despite her high intelligence. Part way through the second session it was clear that her parents were being far too strict with her. She was expected to babysit for her six-year-old sister every day after school without compensation or even verbal appreciation. Moreover, before the marijuana bust, she had been grounded from all social activities for a month as punishment for cutting a class to be with friends. In general, Priscilla's parents were unaware of the kinds of rules and consequences that make sense for teenagers.

In family therapy, they learned to moderate their limit setting by being more positive, less punitive, and providing consequences that were more closely tied to Priscilla's behavior. And the more they respected and listened to their daughter's feelings, the less angry, more compliant, and happier she became.

Although some parents adopt an authoritarian style simply because that is how they were raised, other parents start out trying to be firm but slip into patterns that are too strict because of fears of "what's out there." Priscilla's parents had been doing a pretty good job until she hit adolescence. Part of their overly strict style was directly related to protectiveness. Twenty-first century parents are frightened, receiving messages every day about how dangerous our world has become. Compared to just a decade ago kids today have more exposure to sex and violence at younger and younger ages, more access to drugs that have become more mind altering and more addicting, more knowledge of the stresses and dangers of the world—they are plugged in more than any other generation in history. No wonder some parents would prefer to handcuff them to their bedposts!

Although it is tempting to try harsh punishment when mild punishment has failed, it is often ineffective. In fact, it can completely backfire since strict punishment brings about compliance in the short run but defiance thereafter. Since no one likes to be ordered around or yelled at, children and teens included, we tend to do what it takes to get someone off our back and privately do whatever we want to do. It inadvertently encourages hiding and lying because the fear of punishment makes the child less likely to turn to the parent as a confidante in times of need. Overly strict parents are also more likely to use spanking or other physical forms of punishment. The cycle of anger tends to escalate and to alienate.

In research by Bahr and Hoffman (2010) at Brigham Young University, teens aged twelve-nineteen were assessed for heavy drinking, defined as five or more drinks at one sitting. Coming from an authoritarian family doubled the risk of heavy drinking. The families that were too soft fared even worse, with teens that had triple the risk. The youth that were least prone to this dangerous behavior were those parents were authoritative, exuding both warmth and limits.

FAMILY RULES

It's not wise to violate rules until you know how to observe them.
-T.S. Eliot

In addition to finding the middle ground in parenting, develop some clearly articulated rules to define what is and isn't allowed in your family. Outlining basic rules and routines helps kids know what is expected of them and what behaviors are out of line. It makes life run smoother *and* lowers children's anxiety to know what's what. Some rules may be implied, like respecting others or being kind, and others spelled out very specifically, such as bedtimes or curfews. Some rules exist for small children; others apply to everyone. As with striking a balance between too soft and too firm, healthy families balance the need for clear rules and consequences without creating so many rules that it's hard to keep track.

If you haven't already done so, you may want to sit down with your parenting partner and write down some rules. The very process of discussing them may lead to some very interesting conversations—and potential conflicts to be resolved. Airing these differences before they become a problem is a wise and prudent endeavor. When stuck, you may want to talk to other parents who are effective at setting limits.

Perhaps the most powerful way parents can teach their kids rules is living by them. There is an old adage that seems to apply well: "What children hear, they mostly forget. What they see, they mostly remember. What they do, they understand and internalize." Although there are some exceptions, the majority of family rules should apply to *everybody*. If the rules are only for the kids, or if they're supposed to be for everybody but you the parent break one, you're in effect saying, "Do what I say—not what I do!" or "Just wait until you grow up. Then you can break all the rules you want." For example, if you make a family rule that everybody's room has to be kept presentable but your bedroom remains a mess, you're sending a mixed message. Rest assured that either your child's room will look the same or that rebellion or resentment will soon be on the loose. The same thing pertains to our manner of speaking to one another.

Rules provide a road map for helping family members get along with each other and with others in the outside world. They fall into several basic categories. First and most crucial are rules that keep children and teens safe. Protection is the reason for teaching small children not to get in cars with strangers and for creating serious consequences when teens drink and drive. If you are trying to change a pattern of permissiveness, start with basic safety rules and go from there.

The second area for rules has to do with respecting other people's boundaries, which include physical space and touch, sensitivity to needs and feelings, and respect for property and privacy. Some common examples: knocking on the bathroom door, not hitting, and asking before borrowing something. Some of these standards of good behavior become long-term projects, requiring intervention in different ways depending on the child's age.

Most families run more efficiently with a clear set of expectations about maintaining a neat and orderly environment. What rules do you have about putting things away, having chores, keeping rooms tidy, noise and activity levels, et cetera? Far too often we see families where both mom and dad work full time jobs yet they are still doing all the housework. What message does it send the children about the importance of sharing responsibilities or pitching in to help, or about everyone doing their part? We are constantly teaching our children values, whether we are doing it consciously or not.

Another arena where most families have rules pertains to

personal responsibilities. Once children begin school, we generally expect them to attend faithfully, to participate as best they can, and to complete whatever tasks or homework they are given. Most parents tell kids that school is like their "job," and just as mom has to be at work on time and dressed appropriately, they have to go to school having had a good night's sleep and a healthy breakfast.

WORKING AS A TEAM

In order for all of this to unfold, parents must be good leaders. They should carry both the responsibility and the authority to effectively carry out the tasks of family life. When there is more than one parenting figure in the home, it is essential that the adults work together as partners, like co-captains of a team. Directing in a reliable and consistent way, parenting partners must also make some decisions behind closed doors. Although input from the children can at times be helpful, parents need to be in charge of the timing and appropriateness of their kids' involvement in the decision-making. Only indulgent parents allow the kids to interrupt, get in the middle, or dictate the terms of their own discipline.

Problems can arise if one parent becomes stuck in the role of "bad guy" while the other takes on the role of "nice guy." Like a seesaw, one parent is progressively more permissive as the other becomes more strict. Although attempting to balance each other, they are actually casting one another as the enemy, blaming their partner for the children's problems. Before long, kids begin playing one against the other, and if the parents are unable to work out their differences, conflict intensifies and everyone suffers.

Rebecca and Sam agreed that they wanted their eight- and ten-year-old boys to stop the bickering, name-calling and physical battles that troubled everyone. The couple hadn't realized that they were working at cross-purposes when they entered family therapy. In one session, Sam asked the eight-year-old to sit in his chair and listen, but Rebecca inserted, "He can listen and play at the same time." Their son didn't move a muscle. Dad's voice got louder. "Sit in that chair, now." It was only when mom agreed with dad out loud that Billy moved to his chair. The couple realized that the kids had been responding to the tiny, subtle ways that their parents weren't being a team.

Rather than putting blame or fault on the other parent, the best solution is for parents to compromise a bit, shifting their weight toward the center of the seesaw. The strict parent needs to bring more love and warmth into their relationship with the children, while the permissive parent must learn to provide structure and set firmer limits. In addition, both parents need to agree on basic family rules and expectations. When surrounded by a positive family atmosphere with reasonable, age-appropriate rules and consequences, children naturally learn proper behavior.

TIPS & TOOLS FOR SETTING LIMITS

Don't worry that children never listen to you; worry that they are always watching you.
-Robert Fulghum

Parents have two primary ways that they influence their children to become the best that they can be. The first is as role models. The second is through effective discipline—providing consistent age-appropriate rules and expectations as well as consequences for misbehavior. Kids need external limits so that they can learn and eventually internalize them, taking them on as their own. A steady repetition of lessons over years facilitates the development of morality and healthy habits of behavior. The fruits of effective discipline are kids who become happy, responsible, self-sufficient and caring adults. Sometimes it seems like a long way between here and there.

Young children, especially, can act as though they are little kings and queens of the universe—in which our job is to meet their every need like slaves. If we fall into this pattern, we do our children a great disservice since little dictators don't make many friends. There is only a brief period of time in a child's life when we should attend to their every need—during infancy. Indeed, a large body of research shows that responsively parenting in this manner in the first six months of life will not make for a spoiled child; it will make for a happy, trusting baby. The issue of discipline becomes relevant after the child is eight or nine months old.

The shift to discipline occurs so that children are gradually socialized to get along with others. Many parents get stuck in the role of servants when their infants become toddlers. To discipline effectively is to make a gradual transition, particularly after that first year. Ideally there is a shift from catering to their every need right away towards helping our children see themselves as important and special, but not self-centered.

As time goes on and our children begin interacting with others, another challenge often arises: they can act one way at home and another way with peers or at school. When misbehavior shows up in one context but not another, we can determine where to target our efforts at change. If the problem behaviors tend to occur at home, chances are the parents are not effectively in charge; if problems are only happening in settings other than home, that raises the possibility that emotional issues are at play and/or parents may be acting too punitively at home. The good news is that such imbalances can often be remedied in a matter of weeks by parents moving to "center" and also learning how to respond more constructively to their children's misbehavior.

If you lecture your kids and explain the same things over and over again, they will likely tune you out. The same is true if you fall into the habit of repeating yourself umpteen times when you want them to do something. The following behavioral principles and procedures can help break these habits.

CHANGING NEGATIVE BEHAVIORS

Parents are the bones on which children cut their teeth.
-Peter Ustinov

Kids misbehave for a variety of reasons: to get their parents' attention, to show their parents how they are feeling, or even to retaliate for having been mistreated. The best way to discourage these negative behaviors is by working from a positive angle. We do this with a lot of love and by supporting or "reinforcing" appropriate behavior. When we devote time and attention to reinforcing positive actions, we decrease the level of conflict, increase our child's self-esteem, and foster warm feelings between family members.

To reinforce children means to praise, thank, smile, hug, or give them something they like. One of the most powerful reinforcements we can offer younger children is our attention. There are also many other non-material reinforcements that work great with kids; try to avoid always having to give them something material. That procedure can become expensive and also lead to a reliance on material things to get them to behave.

The use of reinforcements is the backbone of effective discipline because it relies on positive rather than negative control. Since parents are such powerful models for their kids, it teaches them to be positive as well. A generally positive approach also reminds our children that they are loved for who they are, and increases the effectiveness of any occasional punishment we use. Our children care more about what we think due to the strengthened bond they have with us. Positive actions with each family member add to the "bank account" of our relationship, whereas negative ones can bankrupt us.

> ### Try to catch your child doing something good and reinforce it!

The use of praise, although a good thing, can be misdirected or overdone. Some parents have been misguided in their attempts to protect their child's self-esteem at all costs. Help your children to feel special and important, but that they are not the center of the universe. Kids who are constantly praised and told how wonderful they are can assume an air of arrogance and over-inflated sense of themselves. Children who are told that they are "brilliant" can mistakenly assume that they don't need to try at things and practice. It is best to praise a child's ability to stick to a task rather than to use labels like "intelligent," "great artist," etc. Teach the importance of practice and effort instead. Children learn best when provided with constructive criticism in the context of a warm and caring relationship.

THE USE OF PUNISHMENT AND PRAISE

Punishments should be given sparingly, and only after trying positive ways of dealing with a situation. If you haven't achieved the 5:1 ratio (positive interactions happening five times more frequently than negative ones), go back to square one and work at that some more. Once this is accomplished you can more effectively use mild consequences or punishments.

In addition to reinforcing desirable behavior, you'll want to devise a strategy for dealing with misbehaviors when they arise. For mild behavior problems, consider ignoring them when they occur. Feed them with your attention and they just might grow. Disregard the behaviors and they can often vanish.

Another effective technique to weaken misbehaviors is to praise a child who *is* behaving in front of one who is not. For example, you might want to thank a child who arrives promptly at the table, rather than scolding the one who is lagging behind and ignoring the call to dinner.

When a negative behavior occurs for the first time, provide a brief explanation to a child as to why it's not okay. Most kids don't need or respond well to repetitive explanations or lectures. If a problem behavior starts to become repetitive and talking solutions have failed, the best strategy is to create a few simple rules with prearranged and agreed-upon consequences. For example, you can let your children know that if they don't finish dinner, they can't have dessert. A consequence of this sort is far more effective—and less exhausting— than trying to convince kids of the importance of a balanced meal or telling them about all the hungry children in India.

One of the best ways to use negative consequences with children is to deprive them of something they like. A mild punishment that connects logically with the problem behavior is usually the most effective. A common and successful example is taking a toy away that is being misused. For teenagers, coming home chronically late can be met with an earlier curfew the next time. This approach minimizes hostile feelings and yet gives the child a way to learn about the consequences of misbehavior.

FINDING AGE-APPROPRIATE CONSEQUENCES

Consequences— and expectations as well—should always be geared to the age of the child. Grounding a five-year-old for a week or making a sixteen-year-old stand in the corner is obviously not the way to go. Every child has unique likes and dislikes that can help you find an effective consequence.

An effective mild punishment for children between the ages of three and eight is a "timeout." Some parents timeout their kids by sending them to their room, but we don't find this to be particularly effective. A child's room can be a fun place to hang out. The "sending to the room" idea can work for times you want them to cool off emotionally, but it is not recommended for dealing with repetitive behavior problems. In those instances the best form of consequence is to timeout a child by having them stand facing a corner for a very short time. The time can range from a half a minute for three-year-olds, on up to a couple of minutes for eight-year-olds. Always give big hugs after they have complied.

For teens and tweens, taking one of their "gadgets" away for twenty-minute chunks of time can be one of the most effective consequences to change behavior—things like Game Boy, computer games, iPod, TV, etc. Taking away small chunks of time is best because you are more likely to use the consequence and follow through. Children who don't care about gadgets can lose a small chunk of time when they aren't allowed to do another kind of favorite activity.

Ideally, consequences should follow as quickly as possible after a problem behavior and be directly related to it, (such as removing the plastic bat a child has used to bash her brother on the head). For two- to five-year-olds, consequences should be almost immediate. Kids from age six to twelve can link the consequence to the behavior if it is given and completed within twenty-four hours of when the problem behavior occurred. Teenagers can handle delays of a week or two, but grounding them for months can often just build resentment rather than accomplishing your behavioral goals.

When mild punishments do not succeed in changing a behavior, reevaluate and select slightly stronger consequences. Like medicine, the punishments we dole out should be strong enough to have an effect, but not so potent as to produce the most common unwanted side effect—lots of resentment. If taking a half-hour of TV away doesn't do the trick for a ten-year-old teasing his sister, try an hour, and so on.

The amount of power that parents hold in the family must shift over time. As young children develop into young adults, they become capable of taking on increasingly more responsibility. We like to link up the notions of responsibility and freedom. The more responsibility your child demonstrates, the more freedom they have earned. Like the keys to the car, you would not want to extend more freedom than your youngster has proven he or she can handle.

A family came for help because the parents were concerned about their thirteen-year-old daughter. She stayed out late at night, was sexually active, and drank alcohol at parties. She started doing poorly in school. This family had many strengths, but home life was complicated by the fact that the parents often traveled out of town together, leaving two teenagers behind without supervision.

The solution was in helping them realize that their daughter wasn't old enough to have so much freedom. The parents agreed that the daughter needed to take more responsibility in her life, and that would be the means for her earning more freedom. With more supervision and parental involvement her negative behaviors turned around, and within a short period of time her grades improved dramatically. Follow-up seven years later showed them all to be doing well.

REDUCING NEGATIVE EMOTIONS

An important reason for the use of incentives and consequences described above is to reduce negative emotions. One of the most common traps that parents fall into is to yell at their children. The strong feelings that we have as parents are very understandable. Nothing can upset us more than an out-of-control ungrateful child who is "in our face." (Somehow they don't seem to factor in all the ways we have sacrificed ourselves for their benefit).

There are other disadvantages of falling into the anger trap. The first is that we are modeling anger and a lack of emotional self-regulation. Remember, we want to be teaching how to have feelings but not let them get the best of us. And as we learned in Chapter 2, emotions are contagious and get spread around.

Secondly, when we get angry with our kids, they tend to "get" us back because they are mad at us. Although their anger won't necessarily get expressed directly, it'll come out somehow—for example by taking their good, sweet time when we're trying to get them out the door quickly. Another way their anger can get directed is at siblings or peers.

What works best is to actually move to a "place" where you don't care so much about how your child is behaving, but simply arrange and stick to the consequences. "Nathan, would you like to pick up your toys like I asked, or would you rather spend some time in the corner?" "Juniper, do you want to stop talking to me like that or shall I take away some time from your TV tonight?" No big drama, no standing over the child, no attachment. The sweet paradox is that the more you *don't* care how your child behaves and let the consequences work, the more your child will start to care and step up to the plate.

Think of the image of the police officer who pulls you over for speeding. Officers don't warn you, scold, lecture, guilt trip, hit you, or repeat themselves. They just give you a ticket. Or if that's not enough, the second one costs even more. That's not a bad model to use as a parent. With the use of consequences we are simply preparing our child for the real world.

TIPS & TOOLS FOR "SCREEN TIME"

Television has changed the American child from an irresistible force to an immoveable object.
-Laurence Peter

We have entered a new age of electronics and mass communication unlike any other generation has ever encountered. Ron Taffel, Ph.D., addresses this issue masterfully in *Childhood Unbound: Saving Our Kids' Best Selves—Confident Parenting in a World of Change* (2009*).* Rather than burying our heads in the sand or lamenting on how the world has gone to hell in a hand basket,

Taffel recommends, as do we, that parents find ways to enter into this brave new world with their children. In the old days, this was not such an issue. Most families had the same rule: you can watch TV or talk on the phone when you've done your homework. TV shows weren't available 24/7 and very few kids had phones in their rooms. It's not so simple anymore...

Parents are wise to establish clear rules about the use of cell phones and computers, establishing guidelines when the children are young. This means deciding how much time per day you want your child to watch TV or play with electronic gadgets, and sticking to it. To make monitoring easier, we recommend that children not have TVs in their bedrooms, but instead locate them in common areas. This keeps the kids from holing up in their rooms where you can't connect with them, let alone know what they are really up to.

SCREEN TIME

Based upon scores of brain and behavioral studies, the American Academy of Pediatrics recommends not more than one to two hours per day of screen time (2001). More than that amount can have negative effects on children's school performance, particularly scores in reading. Research on ten- and eleven-year-olds found that children allowed more than two hours of daily screen time were sixty-one percent more likely to have social and emotional problems (Page, et al., 2010).

Just as the Internet has opened up both extraordinary amounts of useful information and uncensored, unprotected sites, there are also good and bad things on television. Children can be damaged by overexposure as well as inappropriate exposure to information, images, and predators on the Internet. In addition to rules about how much daily time is allowed, it is helpful to establish guidelines about what kind of programming is appropriate given the age of your child.

Another reminder about how imitative children are: if you want your kids to be doing things other than watching TV, talking on the cell phone, or being on the computer, you may have to start by monitoring and changing your own behavior. Don't keep the TV on at all times or talk or text on the cell phone at dinner. In fact, we recommend electronic-free times when the family just hangs out together—such as during mealtimes, at family outings, or after a certain time of day or evening.

Many teens have confided in us about how they text their friends into the wee hours of the night. They feel anxious with the threat of feeling even momentarily disconnected from their "tribe" of peers. For some kids this pattern is problematic and requires more monitoring and limits. It also works well to empathize with how hard it can be to feel cut off from their friends.

When it comes to computer and videogames, there is also evidence that certain children and adults have an addictive tendency that makes this form of activity a serious problem. We have seen kids and adults who have flunked out of school, lost jobs, and lost relationships because of their obsession with gaming. Developing healthy habits is easiest done day by day from childhood on.

SETTING LIMITS IN SINGLE PARENT FAMILIES

Single parents, despite merciless attacks in by the media in recent years, are perfectly capable of being in charge and setting effective limits. In fact, many single parents are far more successful at it after separating from a partner with whom they have been at odds. Whether there are one, two, or four parents involved, the reigning principle remains the same: adults need to be clear, firm, and in charge.

Single parenting does, however, entail unique challenges. Unless you are surrounded by an actively participating extended family or community, your parenting job lasts twenty-four hours a day, seven days a week, with no paid vacation or retirement benefits! Consequently, to avoid getting worn out you'll need to take plenty of time to nurture yourself and refuel. Self-care for a parent, especially a single parent, is never a selfish act. On the contrary, it is a necessary ingredient of a healthy family life and hence one of the greatest gifts you can give to your kids.

Another challenge for single parents is a sustainable income. Far too many single parent families, particularly those with female heads of household, are at a severe economic disadvantage in our society and are falling below the poverty line. Until our nation prioritizes the well-being of its children's caretakers, they must make do as best they can.

It can complicate the situation in a single parent household when children try to fill the shoes of their missing parent. Although taking on such added responsibility can be beneficial to both the child and the family, this "parentification" of the child must remain tempered because a child deprived of age-appropriate activities can suffer significant social and emotional setbacks. If granted power over younger siblings, they may also end up bearing the brunt of sibling resentment and other negative emotions. In the final analysis, when it comes to setting limits, the adult must still be in charge.

Some single parents struggle with setting limits with their children out of feeling sorry for them that they have an absent parent. Relaxing the rules a little can be helpful in the short run when a child has experienced big losses, changes or is sick, but a return soon after with appropriate rules and limits will limit disruption in the long run.

When single parents don't have enough outside social support and friendships, it often makes it harder to set limits with their kids. They can be relying too much on their kids for the closeness they seek, and if they set limits, their kids might be mad at them—a condition that no parent can afford to fear.

SETTING LIMITS IN STEPFAMILIES

When two families come together, or "blend" into a stepfamily because a new adult relationship has been formed, additional complications arise about who's in charge. For example, many stepchildren spend part of the week with dad and his new wife, part of the week with mom and her new partner, part of the week with grandparent caretakers, and several hours a week with a babysitter. Children exposed to so many different arrangements often get confused about the rules, and all the more so if the adults have problems communicating with one another.

Although current research suggests that a higher percentage of children from divorced families than from intact families need psychological help, most remain healthy. Constance Ahrons, in her book *The Good Divorce* (1994), examined the long-term research on divorced families and found that many of these children do *not* suffer serious long-term consequences. A crucial difference between a "good" and "bad" divorce from the standpoint of children is the adults' willingness to work together as co-parents. The overriding message is that if there are two houses and four co-captains, the adults must pull together in cooperation. The effort is well worth the energy it takes for the sake of the children.

Stepfamilies also give rise to "divide and conquer" tactics. It's amazing how creative kids can be with power plays when mom and dad live in two different places. We have witnessed a variety of dramatic ways that kids act under these circumstances, even though they may not be conscious of what they are doing. Favorites include threatening to run away to the other parent's home; divulging partial truths about the other parent's rules, making them seem overly strict or inappropriate; and sweet-talking one parent into greater leniency because of the other's alleged meanness. It comes as no surprise that difficulty with a new partner's children is the number-one reason many second marriages end in divorce. Setting appropriate limits is a critical dimension of success.

TIPS & TOOLS FOR STEPFAMILIES

Problems with kids in stepfamilies happen a lot when you are hearing only your child's perspective on things, instead of speaking directly with your ex-partner. Start a "rumor control" program. Don't assume anything negative about the other household without communicating with the other adults in an open, nonjudgmental way.

When couples are experiencing a lot of conflict in the divorcing process, children can obviously become victims of the tensions. What is less apparent, but very important, is how children can also be participants in fanning the flames of that conflict. One example of this was a mom who believed her ten-year-old son when he reported that her ex hadn't fed the boy all weekend and his refrigerator had "nothing in it." Mom had to exercise great restraint not to call her attorney and further fan the flames of their divorce war.

Work together as a team with your ex-partner to create common guidelines for the "big" rules, acknowledging that every household has its own idiosyncrasies. For example, insist on agreements about school attendance, bedtime policies, rules for respect, and similar consequences for misbehaviors. Less important are variations between houses on snacks, mealtimes, or even policies about chores.

As far as your new family goes, don't expect your children and new partner to like each other too quickly. The biological parent should be the disciplinarian when it comes to rules and consequences. Children accept limits far better from someone with whom they have a loving, long-term bond, and you don't want to taint your new partner with the upset feelings kids can have about this "stranger" who's telling them what to do.

Reach out for information and support. Read books and magazine articles about co-parenting. Also check out local stepfamily support groups and parenting classes in your area.

WHAT ABOUT SPANKING?

Any child can tell you that the sole purpose of a middle name is so he can tell when he's really in trouble.
-Dennis Fakes

Parenting experts discourage the use of spanking and other forms of physical punishment, viewing these as both harmful and unnecessary. Despite this, a high percentage of parents still spank their kids. The primary *disadvantages* of spanking are the following:

1. It sends the message that a good way to get what you want is to use physical force or violence. Kids who are spanked at home tend to use this model for working out their differences with others, regardless of any advice we may give. Why? Because they are far more likely to do what we do than to do what we say.

2. Spanking provokes angry feelings that the child may direct toward peers, siblings, pets—or, more than likely, back at you. Resentment builds up until it is unleashed, often in an altogether different context.

3. Hitting your children can damage their self-esteem. Since kids identify so closely with their bodies, spanking leaves them with the impression that *they* are bad rather than that their behavior is unacceptable. To be happy and healthy, children need to feel good about themselves and know that they are loved even when their behavior is not.

Considering the harmful side effects, all of which have been widely publicized in the media, why do so many parents still spank their kids? The simplest explanation is that in the absence of new models, most of us repeat history. Physical punishment also gives the illusion of being effective because it can abruptly stop unwanted behaviors. Trapped in the moment, we become too myopic to see the bigger picture involving the build-up of anger and other long-term side effects.

Another reason why parents continue to spank their children is to vent their own frustrations. Once we have learned how to deal with our negative feelings in healthier ways, as is described in Chapter 2, we take care of ourselves but no longer at the expense of our children.

Parents from all walks of life have made a shift away from spanking. In reshaping their approach to discipline and adding doses of positive reinforcement, these parents have not only corrected problems, but greatly enhanced harmony and good feelings for the whole family. Even some of the most out of control kids imaginable can respond well.

IF YOU DECIDE TO MAKE A SHIFT

If and when you decide to revise your approach to discipline, give your kids some advance warning. Hold a family meeting to talk over the changes you would like to make. They need informed consent. Ask them what they would like to change. As much as they are able and willing, include them in the creation of new rules, reinforcements, and consequences. Subsequent family meetings can be helpful to reevaluate your approach. Additional procedures will be covered in Chapter 12, Making Changes.

If you have discovered a need for some help with this Key, there are a number of excellent books in our section on Self-Help Resources that describe appropriate behavior and methods of setting limits at each stage of childhood, from infancy through adolescence. You also may want to consult with other parents of children the same age as yours.

Now that you better understand the nature of this Key, you may want to go back and re-score yourself in the Current Family Assessment.

KEY #5 TIPS: WHO'S IN CHARGE

- Practice large doses of love and warmth *with* lots of firmness and structure.
- Include your children's input on goals and tactics, particularly with changes.
- Use positive encouragement and praise far more often than negative words.
- Use consequences for misbehavior rather than scolding, lecturing, and yelling.
- Praise a child's effort rather than use superlative labels like "You're a great artist."
- Catch your child doing something good and reinforce it.

CHAPTER SIX

KEY # 6
BALANCING CLOSENESS
AND DISTANCE

Love one another, but make not a bond of love:
Let it rather be a moving sea between the shores of your souls.
Fill each other's cup but drink not from one cup.
Give one another of your bread but eat not from the same loaf.
Sing and dance together and be joyous,
But let each one of you be alone.
Even as the strings of a lute are alone
Though they quiver with the same music.

Give your hearts, but not into each other's keeping.
And stand together yet not too near together;
For the pillars of the temple stand apart,
And the oak tree and the cypress grow not in each other's shadow.
-Kahlil Gibran

Since infants are entirely dependent on adult caregivers to survive, we are born with a biological need for closeness, touch, and nurturing. In the great majority of people, this desire persists from birth to death. Psychologist John Bowlby described and explained the universal need for secure relationships or bonds between young children and their primary caregivers, calling it "attachment theory" (1958).

Our early experiences of bonding are critical to our later desire and capacity for intimacy as adults. Attachment theory is built into most models of therapy, especially when focused on our intimate bonds. Relationships that frequently satisfy the desire for intimacy and connection lead to more secure bonds between partners or between parents and children. On the other hand, relationships that rarely satisfy the desire for closeness lead to less secure attachments. Children and adults almost universally prefer to be with close family members at times of distress, illness, or pain.

From birth until around the age of two, babies crave touch and connection and learn the ability to form positive trusting connections with others. This first phase of closeness gives way to increasing desires for distance and freedom to explore. The two- or three-year-olds favorite new words are "Mine" and "No!" and "I do it by myself!" Lively tantrums often follow when these bids for more autonomy are ignored or denied.

This ongoing tension between the need for closeness and the simultaneous need for autonomy is a necessary part of normal childhood development. The young toddler's movement away from the safe arms of the caregiver fuels new learning. Exposure to new and increasingly complex experiences forges new and necessary pathways in the developing brain. If we want to raise competent and happy children, we must respect their persistent need to learn to do things for themselves: to lead and to follow, to soothe their own emotions, to amuse themselves independently of others as well as to cooperate.

Couples go through a similar process when developing closeness. When people fall in love and bond with a new partner, they crave more intimacy and connection. This stage usually gives way, sooner or later, to a time of more frequent conflict that in turn creates the development of more autonomy and distance. Anyone who has been in a serious relationship can describe just when each knew that the "honeymoon" was over. This potentially painful phase is the grown-up version of saying "No" and "What about me?" and reflects the growing need for independence that naturally follows when the bond feels secure.

We have each shared this story many times with couples going through the often-stormy stage of evolving autonomy. (Think terrible twos for a couple...) When we first started living together, we had two hugely ridiculous fights...one, over where to keep the vacuum cleaner and the other about where exactly the rug should be placed in the living room! People laugh at our story, realizing how on the one hand, these were such trivial things to be fighting about, and on the other hand, how anything can be fought over when exerting one's desire for power and autonomy. Each of us, we explain, was letting the other know we were not going to lose ourselves in this relationship. —Debra and Don

The sixth Key to a happy, loving family is integrating and accepting the ongoing existence of these two competing needs— for closeness *and* for distance—in each and every member of the family. Neither attribute is better or more important or more functional. In fact, you can't really have one without the other. The second part of this Key is the awareness of how these two competing needs change over the course of the family life cycle.

BALANCING CLOSENESS AND DISTANCE IN THE FAMILY

We need to be sometimes alone and sometimes together. We're afraid of distance, and also afraid of close relations. We run from distance to relations and from relations to distance. We need to learn to choose: Sometimes distance, and sometimes relations without fear. Without distance there is no dialogue between the two.
-Martin Buber

The sense of connection, sometimes called "family cohesion" describes the emotional bonding that family members have with one another. All the major schools of family therapy acknowledge this as a factor that distinguishes healthy from dysfunctional families. Some of the specific variables used to diagnose and measure the family cohesion dimensions are: emotional bonding, boundaries, coalitions, time, space, friends, decision-making, and interests and recreation. The crucial element for families is how they balance their separateness versus togetherness. Most models of therapy address this issue although with different names such as dependency versus codependency, enmeshment and disengagement, or levels of individuation.

It's all about balance. There is a problem in either extreme—in families with very low levels or very high levels of cohesion. Optimal family functioning includes adequate amounts of emotional connection and adequate amounts of emotional autonomy mixed together in different combinations across the span of the life cycle.

In an ideal family, individuals feel emotional closeness, loyalty, and connection with other family members shown through empathy and knowledge of one another's lives, regular time together, shared activities and information, expressions of warmth and love, play and touch. At the same time, family members get the encouragement to be unique, independent individuals—to act on their own as is developmentally appropriate, think for themselves, form their own opinions, and have their own feelings and preferences. Each person is seen having a particular set of strengths and weaknesses, gifts and liabilities, temperaments and issues.

This balancing act between closeness and distance is necessary for couples as well. A couple is made up of two individuals who have a strong bond and connection but still possess two separate voices and are therefore able to agree and disagree. A connected relationship has emotional closeness and loyalty to the relationship. There is a priority put on togetherness. Time together is equally important as time alone. There are separate friends, but also friends shared by the couple. Shared interests are balanced with separate activities.

As a couple we work several days a week together and share in the direction of the nonprofit agency that we run. Although we are very close, it is also imperative that we have significant chunks of time apart. I am a professional songwriter of children's music and lock myself away for hours in the studio. Debra escapes into a world of art, beading, and a voracious appetite for reading. Sometimes we'll turn to each other and quite lovingly encourage the other to take off for a while so we'll have a chance to miss each other! –Don

The way each of us learns about closeness and distance begins in our childhood families, although the "rules" about boundaries are often not explicitly spelled out. As a result, this balancing act between autonomy and connection and which end of the teeter-totter we prefer can be unconscious. The first step is to bring awareness to this issue by asking yourself some questions. Do the adults in this family get any alone time or time away with friends? Or perhaps one or both adults take too much time away from the family? As a couple, do you get time alone for "dates" or is the whole family together all the time? Are children able to respect the right of parents to be alone and make certain decisions behind closed doors? Are the kids capable of spending time alone or are they constantly trying to involve an adult in everything they do? Does your family demonstrate too much closeness or too much distance or just the right dose of each?

TOO MUCH CLOSENESS

We keep only that which we set free.
-Chinese origin

In relationships characterized by too much closeness, individuals are overly dependent on each other. There is a lack of personal boundaries and little private space is permitted. Emotions are highly contagious in these types of families. In some cases children can easily be frightened by their own need for independence if they sense that their mom or dad is in a panic when they are out of sight. If one person is sad or angry, everyone else's mood is affected. In contrast, in a family with better boundaries one member can have a bad day and others can still be happy.

The sense of "we-ness" overpowers the sense of "I-ness" when family loyalty requires the sacrifice of individual needs to the group. The energy of the individuals is mainly focused inside the family. We have seen enmeshed families who finish each other's sentences, use the word "we" more than "I" when describing themselves, and feel that taking alone time is a betrayal to the others. There is very little separateness; time together is more important than time alone; there may be few if any individual friends or activities, and personal decisions are forced to take a back seat.

One of our favorite funny stories from the early days of our clinic was about a single-parent mom. After gently helping her to understand how over-involved she was with her son, she laughed and proudly proclaimed that she could even feel the pain in her gums when he went to the orthodontist and got his braces tightened!

Sometimes in the very same family with insufficient boundaries between members, there can be overly rigid boundaries keeping the outside world from intruding. Family members can have too few outside individual friends or interests. What goes on within the family is seen as private, and outside influences are limited to those approved. When connection levels are very high, there is too much demand for conformity within the family and too little independence.

Families where there is over-involvement often have difficulties with physical or psychosomatic illness, and children are typically inhibited (even if in very subtle ways) from progressing along the developmental continuum in a "normal" fashion. They can begin to hold themselves back, sacrificing their autonomy to respond to needs that they perceive in the family. From a clinical standpoint, over-involvement can also lead to "spoiling" a child who can then feel too self-important and ignore the needs and feelings of others.

HEALTHY BOUNDARIES

The adult relationship in healthy families is protected by a boundary where certain topics and decisions are kept separate from the children or from the grandparents. A great metaphor is a house with doors that can be open or closed, locked or unlocked. Family members respect closed doors and knock before entering. Children need their own space as well. It is fine for parents to have privacy and lock their bedroom door for more intimacy, but doors are only closed some of the time. For the majority of the time, parents and children have free access to one another and find many "open doors" for shared enjoyment and mutual problem solving.

Ideally there is also a balance around what kind of information is shared with children. Once again, not too much and not too little should be out in the open. Obvious taboos for parents are talking in front of children about your sex life, financial troubles or other juicy topics. On the other hand, given what we have learned about mirror neurons and emotions, it is near impossible and actually damaging to try to keep certain things secret in families. Consider the following example:

> A couple was a hundred percent convinced that their teenage
> daughter, Sylvia, was unaware of their marital difficulties. They
> were great parents in terms of the quality of time and attention they invested
> in her, but Sylvia's health was deteriorating. One day she and her mom
> were driving home from a frustrating appointment where yet another doctor
> could find no physical cause for her illness. She turned to her mom in tears
> and said "Are you and dad all right?" The couple was flabbergasted that
> Sylvia was aware of the marital tension. Sylvia had been confused by
> conflicting messages between how they acted and what she felt in her gut.
> She was relieved to have validation for what she had been sensing all along.

CREATING MORE AUTONOMY

The reason why some families or individuals are more likely to get stuck having "too much closeness" and others by "too much distance" often has to do with the way we were each brought up in the family of our childhood. Our early attachments have helped form our internal concept of just what love and intimacy feels like. If you have discovered that you may be stuck in patterns of too much family closeness and not enough autonomy, here are some suggestions:

First, understand that fear is a common companion to people struggling with letting go. You may be over-involved with your children as a result of something you were taught as a child. Perhaps you received messages such as, "It's not safe to let go or else you can lose someone," or "You will be hurt or punished if you push for freedom." These messages, often learned early, can be floating around under the radar in our unconscious, yet influencing us nonetheless.

Another common pattern of over-involvement can develop for parents of a child born prematurely or with early health problems or disabilities. It makes sense for a parent with a sickly infant to provide extra attention and support. The challenge occurs when that parent, still living with frightening memories from the past, remains over-involved with that child years later. Breaking this pattern may require some help with processing those feelings.

Although people *can* benefit from gaining insight and learning how a problem started, learning "why" doesn't necessarily help. Sometimes there are hidden benefits from our current family patterns that are essential to discover and change. We may think that we want to change, yet seem to be stuck.

A single parent mom was so over-involved with her ten-year-old son that he sat on her lap most of the first session. His symptoms included a seeming inability to do his homework without her sitting next to him, and numerous other examples of his wielding too much power. Most recently he had chased her around the house with scissors when she "had the nerve" to be on the phone for ten minutes.

Although the pattern of too much closeness originated out of mom's guilt about the divorce and disappearance of her ex, there was another explanation that still fueled the problem. I asked her what challenges she might have to face if her preoccupation with her son magically went away. After some deliberation she said she might have to start dating again, "get a life," and or go back to school. She could only set better limits and boundaries after she faced her fears of these personal challenges and no longer needed her son to distract her.

TOO MUCH DISTANCE

At the other extreme, some families "do their own thing" with limited connection or commitment between family members. Relationships are distant and disengaged, characterized by extreme emotional separateness. There is little involvement between each other; individuals are granted a great deal of personal space and independence. Separate time, private space, and separate interests predominate; and members rarely turn to one another for support and problem solving. Instead of feeling like a family, members are more like roommates living under the same roof. There is a lack of cohesion, togetherness, and commitment between parents and children leading to feelings of "What the hell, 'cause nobody cares."

At the same time, in these more distant families, the children often have few boundaries or demands placed on them. They are often insufficiently supervised and may spend large amounts of time alone or away from the family. One common version of this in the past was "the latchkey child." Families with this pattern often wind up with adolescents who are under-supervised and get in trouble. When these teens act out, it can be seen as a desperate attempt to get attention, even if negative, when appropriate closeness and time together are lacking. Sometimes we call it "looking for limits in all the wrong places"! With more and more dual career parents spending fewer hours at home, this pattern is increasingly common.

CREATING MORE CLOSENESS

Fear can be the culprit that keeps us from getting close. We have some favorite questions for couples who struggle along these lines: "When you think about the parents' relationship when you were growing up, how close did they allow themselves to be?" or "How would you compare the closeness that you have with your current spouse or partner to the closeness that your parents modeled for you?" The same set of questions can be asked about closeness of parents with the children as well.

The answers to these questions often help couples see the ways that they have expanded their capacity for closeness beyond the models their parents provided. Some additional questions help couples understand how their relationship with each of their parents has become their template. "How would you describe the nature of your relationship with each of your parents?" or "What was the quality of closeness or distance *you* had with each of them when you were growing up?"

Fears that our parents carried can easily become our own. One client was seeking help for her fear of spiders, although she had personally never had a frightening experience with them. She did, however, have a distinct memory of seeing her mother flinch at the sight of a spider on the ceiling.

In a similar fashion, as children are growing up they can learn "by osmosis" their parents' fears of being too close. Perhaps they saw their parents in open conflict or frequently withdrawn from one another. That child can easily come to believe that intimacy is unnecessary or even dangerous, and later, as an adult, carry that fear into their own relationships. Other forms of programming about intimacy are much less subtle such as, "My mother used to tell me all the time that you just can't trust men."

Developing our capacity for intimacy can be like developing a muscle. It requires a lifelong process of working at it, as well as facing and expressing our fears about possible loss. If you really let yourself love someone, you can also secretly resent them. Your caring so much makes you vulnerable. They could leave you, get run over by a bus, say mean things, or hurt you in a myriad of ways. It is natural to feel this resentment and also helps to "own" the vulnerability by expressing it. We'll even suggest to couples that they gaze into each other's eyes at times and proudly proclaim, "You scare the heck out of me!" Normalizing and expressing these feelings is an important step towards making sure that the feelings aren't acted out unintentionally.

WHAT IS YOUR ATTACHMENT STYLE?

Now that we have looked at patterns of closeness and distance, let's go back to the early roots of bonding and attachment. Each of us are shaped not only by our inborn temperament but by our early environment as children. Attachment theory, as described in the beginning of this chapter, was first used to describe healthy or secure attachments between parents and babies. As this perspective was examined in more depth, psychologists noticed that the relationship we have as children with our primary caretaker is highly predictive of the kind of intimate bonds we form as adults (Ainsworth, et al., 1979). Our "attachment style" can be positive or negative, described as secure or insecure, and will affect both our ability to be close and to be independent in our adult relationships.

CHARACTERISTICS OF SECURE ATTACHMENT

Children who are securely attached have received consistent and prompt attention to their needs as infants. They clearly prefer parents to strangers, and when frightened, will seek comfort from their parent or caregiver. They are able to separate from caregivers with minimal distress, and they greet the return of a parent with a positive reaction.

Parents of securely attached children tend to play more with their children. They are generally more responsive to their children than the parents of insecurely attached children. Studies have shown that securely attached children show more empathy for others during later stages of childhood. These children are also described as less disruptive, less aggressive, and more mature.

As adults, those who are securely attached tend to have trusting, long-term relationships. They would describe themselves as comfortable with depending on others and being depended upon. This style of attachment usually results from a history of warm and responsive interactions with parents or significant adult models. "Securely attached" people tend to have positive views of themselves and their partners. They also tend to have positive views of their relationships. They tend to report greater satisfaction and adjustment in their relationships than people with other attachment styles. Securely attached people feel comfortable with intimacy *and* autonomy and seek a balance of both.

Clearly it should be the goal of anyone raising children to form secure attachments. If you are a new parent or about to be, you will see how important this foundation is for your child's development. We describe the various kinds of insecure attachments next. You may have had parents who were absent, alcoholic, abusive, or simply lacking information on how to create secure attachments. Or you may be married to someone who desperately wants to be a good parent but was not securely attached as a child. It takes some effort to keep the lessons we learned as children from becoming patterns we perpetuate or re-create as parents or partners.

CHARACTERISTICS OF AMBIVALENT OR ANXIOUS ATTACHMENT

Children who are ambivalently or anxiously attached tend to be extremely suspicious of strangers. They have typically received inconsistent early care giving. These children display considerable distress when separated from a parent or caregiver, but do not seem reassured or comforted by the return of the parent. In some cases, the child might passively reject the parent by refusing comfort, or may openly display direct aggression toward the parent. As these children grow older, teachers often describe them as clingy and overly dependent.

As adults, those with an ambivalent or anxious attachment style are often preoccupied with their relationships. They feel reluctant to get too close to others but want to be completely emotionally intimate. They feel caught between a rock and a hard place, both wanting and fearing intimacy. People with this style of attachment seek high levels of approval from their partners. They sometimes value intimacy to such an extent that they become overly dependent or clingy with partners.

Compared to securely attached people, people who are anxious or preoccupied with attachment tend to have less positive views about themselves. They can doubt their self-worth and blame themselves for their partner's lack of responsiveness, or feel untrusting of their partner's love and intentions. They can also exhibit high levels of emotional expressiveness and worry which can lead to frequent breakups or impulsive actions. These individuals are very distressed at the ending of relationships. As adults, they may cling to partners or extended family members or form overly close relationships with the children.

CHARACTERISTICS OF AVOIDANT ATTACHMENT

Children with avoidant attachment styles typically received very little or no response to their distress as infants, as well as discouragement of crying. They were encouraged to be independent much too early. They tend to avoid parents and caregivers, and their avoidance becomes especially pronounced after a period of absence. These children might not reject attention from a parent, but neither do they seek their comfort or contact. Children with an avoidant style often show no preference between a parent and a complete stranger. As adults, those with an avoidant style tend to have difficulty with intimacy and close relationships. They are likely to describe themselves as self-sufficient and prefer not to depend on others or be depended on. People with this attachment style desire a high level of independence. These individuals do not invest much emotion in relationships and experience little distress when a relationship ends. They view themselves as self-sufficient and often deny needing close relationships. They avoid intimacy by using excuses such as long work hours.

Other common characteristics include a failure to support partners during stressful times and an inability to share feelings, thoughts, and emotions with partners. People with a dismissive-avoidant attachment tend to suppress and hide their feelings, and they tend to deal with rejection through distance. As parents, they may have difficulty forming close enough bonds with the children.

CHARACTERISTICS OF DISORGANIZED ATTACHMENT

Children with a disorganized or fearful attachment style show a lack of clear attachment behavior. The word disorganized means that there was not a clear positive attachment but also not a clear negative attachment formed with the parent. As a result, their actions and responses to caregivers are often a mix of behaviors, including both avoidance and resistance. These children are often described as looking dazed, sometimes seeming either confused or apprehensive in the presence of a caregiver. Since the parenting style that goes with this is very inconsistent, the children seem like deer caught in the headlights. Confusion is often the result if a child feels both comforted and frightened by the same parent.

As adults, those with this style have mixed feelings about close relationships. They describe themselves as uncomfortable trusting or getting too close or dependent on others. These mixed feelings are combined with negative views about themselves and their partners. They commonly view themselves as unworthy of responsiveness from their partners, and they don't trust the intentions of their partners. Still wanting closeness yet fearing it, people with a fearful-avoidant attachment style seek less intimacy from partners and frequently suppress and hide their feelings. Adults raised with this style can have great fears or difficulty being consistent as parents.

LIFE CYCLE CHANGES

Shifts between an individual's needs for closeness and distance are constantly changing and evolving. There can be no easy, straightforward set of steps leading to a moving target. What is "normal" at one stage of development may not be so at another. What one member of the family needs may be exactly the opposite of what another is most wanting during that same phase. Infants and small babies thrive on closeness, which is why parents have things like snugglies, slings, and backpacks to attach the baby to their bodies. In contrast, how many minutes can an active three-year-old spend in a stroller or grocery cart without trying to hurdle themselves into freedom?

In the stages of the life cycle, beginnings and endings increase a need for more connection. We've already mentioned how intimacy is the glue that bonds a couple at the outset and takes them through a phase of dating to being more committed. Similarly, births, weddings, illness, and deaths all tend to bring the family closer and can force the necessity of pulling together, spending more time and making more decisions together. In contrast, there are times when more independence is needed; when young children leave the nest to go off to school, when they become teenagers, when young adults leave home, or when the empty nest finally happens. All of these junctures call for more independence for the children and the task of letting go for the family.

Just because someone has left the nest doesn't necessarily mean they are any less connected, especially in this day and age. We have had the opportunity to work with a number of local college students. All too obvious is the influence that friends and peers can have on a student's ability to study and perform well. What is less well known is how tuned in students can be to the troubles their families might be having back home. All too often these students "sacrifice themselves" and get in trouble in a way that catapults them back home to the rescue.

The vast majority of families that turn to us for professional help come at these developmental turning points where change is being demanded. The most difficult transitions happen when the needs of the adults and those of the children are directly at odds with one another. A common example is when a new partner joins a family with a teenager. Imagine the scene where a single parent of a teen begins seriously dating or marries for the second time. The newly forming couple needs to spend time with each other and with all the children in order to form bonds of connection. The teenager wants to have increased independence and time away from the family to sprout wings. No surprise that families call us when a full-scale revolt of the children is about to drive the couple to split up.

Marriages go through similar stages, often in response to the varying needs of the children. After going through an early phase requiring intimacy, the birth of babies often brings distance to the couple now burdened with extra responsibilities together as well as the need to bond with the baby. When the children reach school age, the couple often yearns for more personal closeness again to recover from the infant years. Teens in the home create stress again for the couple, sometimes coinciding with midlife or menopausal issues for one or both adults. After launching kids, the couple may need to recalibrate their intimacy yet another time. Caring for aging parents requires connection with the family of origin again and—again—another balancing act for the couple.

Now that you better understand the nature of this Key, you may want to go back and re-score yourself in the Current Family Assessment.

KEY #6 TIPS: BALANCING CLOSENESS AND DISTANCE

- Find a balance between closeness *and* distance with each member of the family.
- Respect each other's needs for independence, but also be available for help and support.
- In addition to time together, allow kids to also spend time by themselves.
- Keep certain topics and decisions separate from the children or grandparents.
- Stay connected to outside family members and friends.
- Take time for "date nights" or other child-free moments.

CHAPTER SEVEN

KEY # 7
ACCEPTING DIFFERENCES

Insight, I believe, refers to the depth of understanding that comes by setting experiences, yours and mine, familiar and exotic, new and old, side-by-side, learning by letting them speak to one another.
-Mary Catherine Bateson

*E*ach of us has the same unspoken wish—to be loved and accepted exactly as we are. We long to be seen and heard, to express our true unique self without fear of embarrassment or reprisal. Given just how extraordinarily different we are from one another in so many ways—looks, gender, intelligence, culture, beliefs, social class, upbringing, and temperament just to begin, this is no small undertaking. **Learning and practicing awareness and acceptance of our differences** is the next Key to happy, loving families.

RESPECTING MULTIPLE VIEWS OF "REALITY"

When I was a child, my mother used to read poetry to me. One of my favorites was The Blind Men and the Elephant written in the 1800s by John Godfrey Saxe. The poem was taken from a Chinese parable dating back to 200 B.C. In the story, which has many versions in different cultures, six blind men want to understand the essence of the elephant. They get into a huge quarrel. The first, on touching the side of the elephant proclaims it to be like a wall; the second, touching the tusk, insists that it is like a spear. The third, touching the trunk, says it is a snake and so on. The moral of the tale is that while each

of them is telling the truth, none of them is right. Each one
holds only one perspective and is "blind" to the whole truth.
So reality, like the elephant, is more complicated than any one
perspective can reveal. I think this poem seeded my lifelong
interest in multiple perspectives of reality. –Debra

The debate about whose version of reality is actually the correct one is something we usually address at the beginning of therapy. We explain that therapy will not be a series of tattled tales that each person in the family reveals so that the therapist, like the great Wizard of Oz, can deliver a verdict of good versus bad or right versus wrong. Instead, therapy is about creating a safe place to listen to each person's experiences, thoughts, and feelings in order to create less conflict and more closeness through mutual understanding.

We like to use those "he said-she said" moments as an opportunity to teach the family about the existence of multiple versions of "reality." We are, each of us, like a blind man with the elephant. The goal is, little by little, to incite more curiosity about the ways in which each member of the family thinks and feels differently from other members of the group. Learning to accept the differences, especially in sensitive areas, comes later once everyone is better at listening without judging, criticizing, or defending their own point of view.

Each person experiences events and communications from a unique perspective. How could we not? Having our own personal version of events is inevitable. But when we assume that our version of events is the only possible or correct interpretation of events, we begin to get into trouble in relationships. We have spent countless hours interceding between couples or between a parent and child debating who said what, who said what first, which remark started the fracas, or who looked angrily at whom. Rather than fooling ourselves into asserting what we "know" about arguable facts, it works better to say what we *think* to be true, allowing others' observations to be true for them. A conversation would sound like, "This is what I remember happened and it made me feel frustrated. What was going on for you? How do you see it?"

It's critical to keep in mind that the way in which we treat differences (of opinion, feeling, belief, style, needs) will determine whether the family is a safe haven for each of the members to express their unique individuality. Without a welcoming perspective, if it is "my way or the highway," family members will begin to keep their true feelings and thoughts to themselves and reach outside the family for acceptance. A child can wind up hiding their unique qualities and special abilities in order to fit into the atmosphere of conformity.

In couples' relationships it is also helpful to convert our expectations into "preferences," telling each other what we would like rather than dictating how it should be. When we feel pushed to conform to the demands of our partner, we often hold even more stubbornly to our position. Paradoxically, our loved ones will often change when we stop pushing. Acceptance provides the fertile ground for growth and change to take place naturally. When couples get stuck in power struggles over who is to blame or who did what, we inevitably ask, "Would you rather be right, or have a close relationship? These are mutually exclusive options."

DIFFERENT TEMPERAMENT TYPES

We all live with the objective of being happy; our lives are all different and yet the same.
-Anne Frank

A sixteen-year-old girl, Sophie, expressed frustration to her younger sister, Michelle, because she felt she had reached out and was shut down in her attempts to make conversation. In a family session "repair kit," Sophie shared, "Yesterday I asked a number of open-ended questions but you gave me a bunch of one-word answers and didn't ask me anything about myself!" The sisters learned that their personality differences had to be factored in to how they approached one another. Sophie was outgoing and verbal, while Michelle was younger, shy, and struggled to express herself. Sophie was reaching out in the way that she would have appreciated someone reaching out to her. (It is common for people to give to others what they would like to receive rather than what the other person might want.) Recognizing their differences and preferences, the girls learned how to tune into each other better.

Researchers began to probe differences in children's temperaments through a longitudinal study begun in the 1950s (Thomas, Chess, and Birch, 1968). Since then, studies confirm that infants are born with certain built-in traits that affect their style of interacting with people, places and things throughout their lifetime (Kagan, 1994). This validates what many parents knew intuitively all along. Although raised in the same environment, children can have vastly different personality attributes. If not from birth, these differences can be quite apparent shortly thereafter, during the first year of life. Recent research is aimed at uncovering more of the specifics of genetically inherited traits.

Here are nine different factors as described by Chess and Thomas (1996) that can combine to form a child's temperament:

1. Activity levels: Is the child always moving or doing something or is he more mellow and relaxed?
2. Rhythmicity: Is the child regular in sleep and eating or more haphazard or difficult to get into a routine?
3. Approach/withdrawal: Does the child shy away from new people, places, or activities, or approach them willingly?
4. Adaptability: Does the child adjust to changes in plans or resist at times of transition?
5. Intensity: Does the child react strongly to situations, positively or negatively, with lots of intensity or react calmly and quietly?
6. Mood: Does the child more often express a negative or more positive attitude? Do the child's moods shift frequently or do they manifest in even-tempered behavior and a predictable frame of mind?
7. Persistence and attention span: Does the child give up quickly when frustrated with a task or keep on trying? Does the child stick with an activity for a long time or tend to get

bored quickly?

8. Distractibility: Is the child easily distracted from what she's doing or does he shut out external distractions and stay with the activity?

9. Sensory threshold: Is the child bothered by stimuli such as loud noises, bright lights, smells, textures of food or clothing, or does he/she tend to ignore them?

These nine traits combine in various ways to form three basic types of temperament. Approximately sixty-five percent of children fit one of the following three patterns; the other thirty-five percent are a combination of the three types. Understanding these patterns allows parents to tailor their responses to each child's personal characteristics. Within each temperament there are strengths and weaknesses. Working with rather than against a child's temperament is far more effective.

Easy or *flexible children* comprise about forty percent of all kids. These are the children that make parents feel like they are really competent as parents. These kids are generally happy, calm, and regular in sleep and eating, adaptable to change and not easily upset. The disadvantage of easy children is that they can pass "under the radar" of a parent who has another more difficult child who is taking lots of time and attention. Under those circumstances many parents carve out and schedule quality time with their easy child.

Difficult, active, or *feisty children* are often high strung, intense, fearful of new people and situations, and easily upset by noise and commotion. They are often fussy and irregular in sleep and eating habits. Since they have difficulty transitioning from one activity to another, it helps to prepare them in advance for what is going to happen. These children need physical activities, exercise and vigorous play to work off their energy and frustrations. Finding areas where they can have choices will help since they often say "no" reflexively before saying "yes." Luckily, this subgroup represents only about ten percent of all children. They often pose far more difficulties for caregivers, and not surprisingly, are often referred for therapy, especially when there is a difficult match between parent and child.

Slow to warm up or *shy, cautious children* represent about fifteen percent of the mix and are relatively inactive and fussy. They tend to withdraw or to react negatively to new situations but gradually accommodate as they are exposed to the same people or places over time. They are calmed by sticking with a routine and need the patience of parents and teachers as they slowly develop their independence and confidence in new situations.

One of the stories we have told hundreds of times is about how completely different our two children were at birth. They had the same biological parents, relatively the same prenatal environments, and were both born at home with midwives. We used a Leboyer bath, with waters warmed to the temperature of the womb, in order to usher each of them into a safe, soothing world. Our first son became calm in the bath and opened his eyes for the first time, just like Leboyer predicted. That son remains to this day as emotionally unflappable as he was in that bath. Our second-born screamed in the bath, only stopping when held tightly to my chest. We nicknamed him Monsieur Le Crie (Mr. Screamer), and he has always been emotionally sensitive and expressive. As parents, we got "one of each" and needed to learn very different languages to honor their uniqueness. –Don

It is important to evaluate your own temperament and that of your partner as well. These nine traits provide insight for adult behavior, too. With added perspective you'll be able to anticipate which kind of child will push your buttons. For example, if you are the "slow to warm up" type and you have a difficult, active child, your tendency may be to avoid that child. The difficult child will only redouble their efforts to get attention from you, which will inevitably backfire. The challenge for parents is to find effective ways to connect with each child while also being in charge and setting boundaries.

LEARNING DIFFERENCES

If we are to achieve a richer culture, rich in contrasting values, we must recognize the whole gamut of human potentialities, and so weave a less arbitrary social fabric, one in which each diverse human gift will find a fitting place.
-Margaret Mead

Close cousins to differences in temperament are differences in learning. The same child can have different patterns of learning at home than at school. Some children are more affected by their immediate environment (lights, noise, etc.) and benefit from either more or less stimulation. Children have varying degrees of response to different social and emotional climates, levels of structure, different motivators, and more or less repetition.

Some kids have more social needs, working better with teams than alone, or benefitting from more one-on-one time with adults. Other children learn more effectively when they are moving rather than holding still. Since children spend so much time in school, it is important that parents find a good fit for them, especially the active child or the cautious child. Easy children are, by their nature, more adaptable to a wide range of environments.

We also know that intelligence comes in many packages. Remembering the information on emotional intelligence, it is not the brainiest kids who are the "smartest" or who will become the most successful in life. Many of the world's great inventors and creative types had difficult temperaments but learned to channel their high levels of activity and intense focus into a goal they became passionate about. Think of Thomas Edison, Leonardo de Vinci, Ernest Hemingway, and Winston Churchill, to name only a few.

Another difference in learning comes from the way we each take in information most effectively. As a visual learner, I use different colored pens to take notes, understand something better when I've seen it, and easily remember faces. Pictures, visual diagrams, and taking notes all help me to retain new information. I also have a hard time learning if my environment is visually cluttered or unappealing. –Debra

Auditory learners take in information far better when listening (lectures, tapes, music) than they do visually (reading and writing). They benefit from repeating words and concepts aloud, so participating in discussions helps cement their learning. If your child is an auditory learner, just reading a book and writing a paper could be deadly. Better to make an oral presentation and listen to the book on tape. Lots of kids (and adults) benefit from being able to dictate papers using the most current dictation software. It is no surprise that children with a "good ear" for music are usually excellent in foreign languages as well.

There are some children and adults who are neither auditory nor visual but are tactile or kinesthetic learners. These are the so-called "hands on" learners that want to touch everything, put things together and solve problems by doing. Not all school environments address the needs of these individuals who need activities such as conducting experiments themselves, doing role-play, or building things to illustrate abstract concepts. These learners need to move around and to have regular breaks to maintain interest. Many boys fall into this category, and can get in trouble or fall behind in school if their activity levels are not high enough. These kids will be hurt the most by the absence of daily physical education in public schools.

CULTURAL AND ETHNIC DIFFERENCES

We all should know that diversity makes for a rich tapestry, and we must understand that all the threads of the tapestry are equal in value no matter what their color.
-Maya Angelou

One of the challenges for families living in a country like the United States, known as "the melting pot," is understanding and respecting the beliefs, customs, and norms of those raised in traditions different from our own. The demographic landscape is changing at an accelerating rate. Interracial marriages were still illegal in fifteen states until a landmark Supreme Court decision in 1967; the same year that Sidney Poitier's controversial movie *Guess Who's Coming to Dinner* brought the issue home. A poll (Pew Research, 2010) found that one in seven couples are marrying someone from a different racial or ethnic background. Whereas in 1990 only 6.8 percent of newly hitched couples married outside their race or ethnicity, that figure rose to 14.6 percent by 2010. These numbers are certain to rise as polls of young adults indicate increasing acceptance of racial and cultural differences.

The United States is currently seeing the biggest rise of immigration rates in one hundred years, bringing unparalleled diversity to our country both racially and ethnically. Ethnicity is defined as a common group ancestry that brings with it shared values, customs, identity and historical continuity. How strongly a given individual identifies with their ethnic background is affected by several variables. Generally, the longer that people are in the U.S., and the more they rise in income and social class, the more they move closer to the dominant value system of the community as a whole. Families that continue to live in ethnic neighborhoods, working and socializing with others from their culture, especially when religion reinforces their value system, are slower to give up their ethnic identities. Another influence on ethnic identity has to do with the reasons a person immigrated. Those who immigrate by choice assimilate more readily than those who are forced to move for political or economic reasons.

Entire books such as *Ethnicity and Family Therapy* (Monica McGoldrick, et al. 2005) have been written on this topic to help both counselors and family members understand the unique challenges that people from varied religious and cultural backgrounds can have. Although the Keys that we have identified have cross-cultural validity, the complexities of cultural traditions can lead to unforeseen conflicts. What is considered appropriate expression of emotion, for example, may be different in an African-American family as compared to a Japanese-American family, and yet again when compared to a WASP (White Anglo-Saxon Protestant) family. Healthy couples and families learn about each other's differences and find ways to acknowledge and honor the traditions and values of varied cultures.

Fascinating new research indicates that many of our well-intentioned efforts to end prejudice and racial stereotyping may have actually backfired. James Moody (2001) at Ohio State University looked at data from 90,000 teens at 112 different schools from around the U.S. He found that the more diverse or racially integrated the school, the <u>more</u> kids self-segregate by race and ethnicity within the school. Clearly the answer doesn't lie in desegregation alone. It appears that the most important factor to help race relations is to keep talking openly about race, starting when children are very young.

Other research has shown that infants as young as six months old can tell the difference between pictures of black babies and white babies (Katz, 2009). This is because our brains are wired to "discriminate," meaning to notice the differences between things. But since race is such a loaded topic, parents often shush their four-year-olds who say such things out loud such as "Why does that man have black skin?" or "Only the brown girls have breakfast at school." This only sends kids the message that something about this topic is bad or unspeakable, which breeds fear and anxiety.

Parents have learned to talk to their children openly about gender ("Girls can become doctors and police officers, not just boys.") Now we need to do the same about race. One study showed that kids in a two-week history class, when taught explicitly about race and historical discrimination, had better attitudes towards blacks than those simply taught facts about famous African-Americans (Bigler, 2009).

GENDER DIFFERENCES

Sometimes I wonder if men and women really suit each other. Perhaps they should live next door and just visit now and then.
-Katharine Hepburn

The differences between men and women have been the topic of investigation, source of confusion, and subject of debate forever. Although research about the brain continues, there may never be agreement about how the two sexes differ and which of those differences are caused by biological factors vs. ways that boys and girls are socialized. As we just discussed, the norms for male and female behavior and what is taboo for one or the other also have tremendous cultural variation. Suffice it to say, the ways that males and females think and act differently can either bring more stress to a family system or be "spice for the broth," depending on the level of acceptance and understanding.

A few of the known differences between men and women have to do with aggression and expression of emotions. Men and boys are generally more quick to show aggression and more likely to express it physically (Buss, 2005). Women are more likely to show their aggression in less overt ways, using verbal aggression or social rejection more often than physical fighting (Simmons, 2002). Deborah Tannen (2007) describes distinct gender differences with communication styles. Compared to women, men are less inclined to face each other and make eye contact, less inclined to express agreement and support while listening, and more likely to jump from topic to topic. Women are more likely to agree, while men are more inclined to debate. Families that acknowledge the subtle and not so subtle differences between boys and girls without judging or making one superior to the other help to create an equal playing field.

SEXUAL ORIENTATION

Remember that you have not only the right to be an individual, you have an obligation to be one.
-Eleanor Roosevelt

Just as with gender differences, the debate over the cause of homosexuality and whether a given individual is born that way has been a long and often contentious exchange. There is no identified single cause for sexual orientation. The latest theories suggest that it is probably a complex combination of genetic, hormonal, and environmental influences that causes an individual to be heterosexual, homosexual, or bisexual. We still have much more to learn on this subject. Nevertheless, sexual orientation is an everyday reality that can be an issue in the lives of many families.

A twenty-year-old student, Jim, came for therapy after a third panic attack landed him in the hospital emergency room. His levels of anxiety were "off the charts" and medication wasn't working. He was an excellent student, had great friendships and a close and loving family. Therapy focused for a while on his tendency to be a perfectionist and too hard on himself, but only helped him slightly.

Jim finally came to the realization that he was gay. It was the last thing in the world that he wanted to admit because his religion taught him that homosexuality was a choice and a sin. He assumed that his parents would never accept him. His parents flew into town for therapy and struggled for weeks, torn between their love for their son and what their faith had dictated. Fortunately for him, they gradually become more accepting and overcame their feelings of intolerance. Follow-up ten years later: Jim is happy, has been in a long-term homosexual relationship for nine years and his anxiety meds are working. He has a great relationship with his parents and they joined a church that was more closely aligned to their new beliefs.

Studies suggest that seven percent of adult women and eight percent of men identify themselves as gay, lesbian, or bisexual (National Survey of Sexual Health and Behavior, 2010). According to the Department of Health and Human Services, an estimated eight to ten million children are being raised in gay and lesbian households (Child Welfare Information Gateway, 2010). Research on the frequency of same-sex behavior in non-Western countries is harder to find. Widespread stigmatization and criminalization of same-sex behavior in many countries prevent gay men and lesbians from openly expressing or admitting their preferences.

Although there is still a lot of prejudice toward homosexuals, increasing acceptance is the clear trend in the U.S. Once deeply hidden and "closeted" from even family, nowadays prominent leaders in many arenas—politics, the media, scientists, artists, religious figures—have gone public. There are now social clubs and support groups in high schools and colleges for gay and bisexual teens. Further education and exposure is still necessary to help families learn to be accepting of differences in sexual orientation in order to avoid conflict and alienation from their loved ones.

RELIGIOUS DIFFERENCES

Out beyond ideas of wrongdoing and right doing there is a field. I'll meet you there.
-Rumi

Although freedom to practice the religion of one's choice was one of the principles behind the founding of America, there is still tension in many couples and families around religious preference. With over ninety percent of Americans identifying themselves with a specific religion, this is not a trivial issue. According to the census, the United States remains primarily Christian (eighty-four percent) of which around twenty-six percent are Roman Catholic, one percent Mormon, one percent Eastern Orthodox and the balance Protestant denominations. Whereas one hundred years ago, a mere four percent of Americans considered themselves non-Christian, by 1995 estimates are around fifteen percent. In addition to the two percent of Americans identifying themselves as Jewish, the growth of practitioners of Hinduism, Buddhism, Islam, and other faiths is bringing rapid change. Four percent of Americans are atheists or agnostics, not believing and/or uncertain about the existence of God (Pew Forum, 2008).

Just as with race, many religions have traditionally prohibited or strongly discouraged interfaith marriages or even dating. This landscape is rapidly changing with higher rates of intermarriage. Most parents and children now think that all religions teach many of the same fundamental principles of human kindness and ethical behavior. As the world changes, so does the assumption that everyone is born into and remains faithful to one religion. In one study, forty-four percent of adults reported a change of faith or denomination from the religion of their childhood (Pew Forum, 2008.) It is important for family members to practice tolerance and open-mindedness. As we will discuss more in the next chapter, the research on healthy families shows that having a spiritual perspective of some kind and believing and contributing to a "higher purpose" is good for families.

Now that you better understand the nature of this Key, you may want to go back and re-score yourself in the Current Family Assessment.

KEY #7 TIPS: ACCEPTING DIFFERENCES

- Turn expectations into preferences; make requests instead of demands.
- Acknowledge and accept differences in temperament and learning style.
- Educate children about differences in race, religion, gender, and sexual orientation.
- Focus on the strengths of individual differences.
- Practice tolerance and open-mindedness.

CHAPTER EIGHT

KEY # 8
SEEING THE POSITIVE

A positive attitude may not solve all your problems,
but it will annoy enough people to make it worth the effort.
-Herm Albright

The eighth Key to happy, loving families is comprised of a set of important beliefs, values and practices that most people, although not all, might identify with their religion or spirituality. It is a philosophy of life or an ethical code that is learned and shared within the family and often supported by a community of like-minded individuals. Children always learn, in one way or the other, for better or worse, about things such as the purpose of life, the reason for suffering, and what it is to be a good person. Character education occurs whether or not such things are ever discussed directly in the household. Parents often learn the hard way about how kids are amazingly adept imitators, doing what we do rather than what we say. What are the values that foster growth, encourage independence, and build loving connected relationships? What are you teaching your children through your everyday actions?

Almost every examination of successful families finds that some form of spiritual practice helps family members in several ways. Our beliefs about the world and human nature are crucial to creating a resilient mindset, an ability to face the inevitable pain and loss in life and still be productive and happy. Our beliefs also help us feel a part of not only our family but of a larger community. Human beings, like other mammals, are social creatures that thrive on touch, communication and connection. Our families teach us about forming friendships, helping others, and finding meaning in a confusing and often painful world.

SEEING THE BEST IN OTHERS

The deepest principle of human nature is the craving to be appreciated.
-William James

Members of happy families share a basic belief that people are mostly good rather than evil. They understand, as an ancient Roman philosopher noted: "To err is human." All of us make mistakes on the way to becoming better people. But the critical lesson in teaching moral behavior, the difference between right and wrong, is that we do not condemn others when mistakes are made. Because making mistakes and hurting those we love is inevitable we need some process to redress our errors, wipe the slate clean, and put the past behind.

Members of healthy families have more positive outlooks about human nature and about the possibility of changing for the better. Research by Barbara Frederickson (2001) shows that cultivating positive emotions such as gratitude and joy can help build psychological resiliency and improved emotional well-being. When people feel good about themselves, they are much more likely to share those good feelings with others.

Healthy family members make the most out of each other's assets and minimize their liabilities. They give each other the benefit of the doubt, assume the best of each other and see the good intentions in other's actions. When the kid spills the milk, it's a mistake, not a misdemeanor. It doesn't necessarily mean "He's out to get you!"

Parents in healthy families also give their kids (and each other) a lot of praise. They think of their child as having *behavior* they'd like to change rather than thinking of the *child* as "bad." They recognize the difference between the person and the pattern of behavior that they see in someone, believing that people are basically good and have good intentions, despite the fact that we all fall short at times.

COMMON ROADBLOCKS TO BEING POSITIVE

I can complain because rose bushes have thorns, or I can rejoice be-cause thorn bushes have roses.
-Unknown

One of the most common blocks to being positive with our children or partner has to do with how we were treated as children by our own parents. Parents who were given little praise and encouragement as children can struggle in their efforts to be more positive. It's so hard to give what you didn't get!

Madeline, a single parent, came seeking help for her daughter who was having behavior problems at home and school. Jessica was seven years old and seemed angry and upset. Madeline told me she'd read "all the books" but still couldn't accomplish her goal of helping Jessica to behave better. She had consistently been using "timeout" with Jessica but it didn't help.

Madeline learned that mild forms of punishment for misbehavior are very important in parenting, but that punishment is only really effective if used in the context of a warm and positive relationship. Otherwise, firm treatment can have the side effect of souring the relationship. Kids get mad when showered with negativity and will do things to get their parents back. It can also become a game of "cops and robbers" where a child enjoys the challenge of who's winning the battle for control. A successful exit from this trap is the use of praise and positives to bring about change.

Madeline could understand the logic and usefulness of such an approach but had difficulty carrying it out. When we discussed her own childhood she got in touch with a lot of anger. "Why should I give all this good stuff to Jessica," she shouted, "when nobody cared about me?" Her awareness and release of these feelings brought the necessary shift to her becoming more centered and capable of giving.

Another common roadblock to being positive with someone appears as a backlog of resentments or unexpressed feelings towards that person. "How can I be nice to you if I'm so upset with you right now?" If that's the case, first use "The Repair Kit" described at the end of Chapter 1, to clear some of the upsets with constructive methods. Then try the positives again.

As mentioned in Chapter 5, we view the accumulation of "positives" in a relationship as a form of money in the bank. When we've made enough "deposits" of this kind, we can tolerate the inevitable "withdrawals" that come with making mistakes or hurting each other's feelings. Generally, the better we feel about ourselves and any given relationship, the easier it can be to accept responsibility for mistakes or our part in a conflict. The importance of a forgiving perspective can't be overemphasized.

TAKING RESPONSIBILITY

God can only help those who do not justify their behavior.
-Hasidic saying

Family members are naturally more capable of taking responsibility when they feel good about themselves. Parents in happy, loving families take responsibility for their personal well-being, taking time to restore a sense of balance and attend to their own needs. When we fail to care for ourselves, physically and emotionally, there is less for us to give to each other and to our children. Learning to love ourselves and other people, not only our children, can translate into one of the best gifts we give to our children.

Taking responsibility also involves the capacity of family members to be accountable for their actions and words. Parents of healthy families are able to admit mistakes and "own" their part of a problem rather than blaming others. They look on mistakes as an opportunity for learning.

 Angela and Pete were a couple with grown children. They struggled with communication problems for years. Therapy helped them express feelings more constructively, yet when either of them fell back into the blaming patterns, they would withdraw from each other for weeks.

It was rarely possible for either of them to say "I'm sorry" so we built that into a homework assignment. Given the task of apologizing to each other every other day for anything they could come up with, they finally broke the old, cold, stubborn pattern.

Family members in healthy families are also unwilling to become victims of other peoples' actions and let others walk all over them. They are assertive and stand up for themselves in a constructive manner. This requires self-awareness as well as an atmosphere of trust, respect, and as we emphasized in Chapter 1, a belief in the value of non-blaming communication.

ALL FOR ONE AND ONE FOR ALL

Let everyone sweep in front of his own door, and the whole world will be clean.
-Goethe

Clinical observation has long shown that families develop certain *patterns* of interacting that become consistent over time. These patterns are established by parents, develop a life of their own, and can bring different facets of each individual to the foreground. Similarly, certain *rules* of the family, spoken or unspoken, have an important influence over the way that family members relate. In addition there are respective *roles* that individuals in the system play as a part of the whole. A family is more than a collection of independent individuals, best seen as a multi-bodied entity. Just as in chemistry, the whole is more than and different from the sum of its parts.

When we live together, the moods or feelings of certain family members can significantly change those of others. The dour mood of one member will permeate the entire group. Think of the impact that a crying infant, a sullen, withdrawn teenager, or a troubled adult can have on the household's happiness. On the other hand, families often report how miraculously things can shift when members choose to express their feelings in a constructive manner. It can serve to relieve the tension for everybody. Recognizing the way we affect each other helps reduce blaming when the "air is thick," and allows us to focus on what we can all do together to make things better. "Who needs to cry around here, anyway?"

Finally, when looking at how household and family responsibilities are shared among family members, recognition of our interconnectedness leads to a relatively equal distribution of the work. Parents in happy, loving families share the load, and also give kids ever-increasing responsibilities as they get older and are capable of assuming them.

We are astonished when we hear from parents that their kids don't help out at home. One fun way to share housework is to crank up the tunes on Saturday morning while everybody pitches in and works together until certain tasks are accomplished. With all hands on deck, a lot can get accomplished in a short half hour. Younger kids like it when the task of cleaning up can also be made into a game to "beat the clock."

> *The routine we evolved as a family, with two adults working outside the home, became a ritual of sharing and connectedness. After our family dinner, which we tried to do on most school nights, everyone would get up from the table at the same time. One of us would clear the table, one would wash off the dishes, another would load the dishwasher while the last was wiping down the counters. We had fun trying to get it done in less than ten minutes. Since we did this every night from the time the kids were four and six years old, there was hardly a complaint. We sent the message that everyone should help so the burden didn't fall on any one person.*
> *–Debra and Don*

THE GOLDEN RULE

The best way you can cheer yourself up is to cheer someone else up.
- Mark Twain

If we accept the fact that everyone wants to be treated with kindness and consideration, then it is certainly a key to happiness in relationships when we can offer such treatment to others. Various forms of the Golden Rule exist in the teachings of over twenty world religions. In Christianity the creed is, "Do unto others as you would have them do unto you." Buddhism teaches, "Hurt not others in ways that you yourself would find hurtful." Judaism teaches, "What is hateful to you, do not do to your fellow man. That is the entire Law; all the rest is commentary." And in Islam, "No one of you is a believer until he desires for his brother that which he desires for himself."

Despite being such an ancient teaching, The Golden Rule closely parallels the latest thinking on how connected we are to one another. We always have the choice in relationships to bring out the best in each other, or not. If we choose a path of punishment or vengeance and try and seek retribution, we only really hurt ourselves. We are all in the same boat.

THE PRACTICE OF FORGIVENESS

Life is a shipwreck but we must not forget to sing in the lifeboats.
-Voltaire

A family came in for help after a mom and dad had a screaming fight that ended in his moving out. Their teenage son got involved by protecting the mom, which led to a shouting and shoving match with his dad. Fortunately, it didn't result in any scratches or bruises, but you can imagine how everyone's feelings were pretty raw.

We had a number of sessions to heal the rift. The dad shared some sincere and heartfelt apologies with his son, but the son wouldn't accept the apology. He wanted his dad to accept one hundred percent of the blame. I explained that the game of finding blame usually serves no useful purpose in healing and helping people get along. The secret to healing wounds lies in our ability to take responsibility and learn from mistakes.

Forgiveness is another fundamental element of happy, loving families—learning to forgive rather than hold on to grudges. Given that we are human and make mistakes, there are inevitable needs for repair of upset feelings. Here are some concepts and action steps that can move you to a genuine place of forgiveness more quickly and effectively.

Hold forgiveness as a goal...a good thing to be attained. We all have a tendency to want to save face when confronted with blame. Each of us has an "ego," a sense of ourselves that wants to be preserved and protected. It is all too easy to see the faults in others while we neglect to take responsibility for our own actions. Discover this blaming part of you and tame it. Don't let it wreck your relationships.

Remind yourself that others "deserve" to be forgiven, just as we do, because people are always doing the best that they can at any given moment. We believe that the actions people take are an inevitable result of the genes they inherited in combination with the life experiences that they have had. In the simplest terms this means if we had been in the other person's shoes, had walked a mile in their moccasins, that even _we_ might have done the same thing under the same conditions. So the question becomes, "Who are we to judge others?" or "Since I am not perfect, how can I expect perfection from others?"

Another concept has to do with "ownership." As we emphasized with the "repair kit" tool, a key ingredient for resolving conflicts is to understand that when we are having upsetting feelings, those feelings are _our_ responsibility to fix, not others. All we can do is change ourselves, so that's where we want to place our attention. If I am upset with you, that's my problem. This is a concept that can break the back of perpetual conflict. Act as if "there's nothing wrong with you that a change in me won't fix." After the tension of the conflict is broken, two people who care about each other can willfully change their actions in order to please other family members and bring out the best in them.

Another key to forgiveness is not to "try" to be forgiving because it's the right or religious thing to do, but rather to get there "honestly." This usually means expressing feelings of hurt and anger first. As we learned in Chapter 2, expressing feelings on our own can move us down the path, then using "I" statements and constructive conversations to handle the rest.

Thus far we have been focusing on the victim of a wrongful action. An additional element of healing can occur when the person who has done something hurtful offers a sincere apology. Successful apologies include taking responsibility for the hurtful actions, a statement of regret, asking for forgiveness and a pledge about future actions. Depending on the situation, restitution can also help. Examples include: If you broke the window, you fix it. If you hit your sister, you do her chores.

Saying you're sorry only works when it's authentic. Don't even go there until the emotional brain settles down. Mouthing words or offering an "empty apology" simply sends red flags to the receiver, whose brain will believe the nonverbal message rather than the words that are spoken. Wait until you can be sincere, and then try to understand the other person's perspective. Authentically resonating to another's pain is an important but often missing step on the path to forgiveness.

SERVING A BIGGER PURPOSE

You don't choose your family. They are God's gift to you.
-Desmond Tutu

Other principles that we learn in families or from religious instruction have to do with the purpose and meaning of life itself. Couples that have a shared sense of purpose feel more connected and happy. Those who persevere through difficult times often share that they have learned something valuable from times of personal hardship.

Our son, Cree, had a mountain biking accident just before his twenty-first birthday. He suffered a head injury that rendered him unconscious for eleven days, followed by many months of slow, painful rehabilitation. He had to relearn how to walk, talk, and function in every way. At the same time as we were immersed in our grief and anguish, we needed to rise to the greatest challenge of our lives—to take care of him and carry on with work and daily responsibilities. We did this by relying on all of the psychological and spiritual tools we had. Now years later, we are happy to report that Cree has made a complete recovery, and more importantly, that he considers his accident to have been both a blessing and great teaching for him. –Don and Debra

The strength to be able to find the silver lining even in times of darkness has inspired many moments of heroism, greater empathy for the suffering of others, and acts of generosity and human kindness. Those individuals who have the ability and the opportunity to be economically or socially altruistic not only leave the world a better place but often feel better about themselves and others.

As the often quoted existentialist philosopher Nietzche said, "He who has a *why* to live can bear with almost any *how*." Viktor Frankl, a psychologist who survived the Auschwitz concentration camp, wrote about how important it is that we find a sense of meaning even in the midst of pain and suffering, and how his sense of purpose and meaning kept him alive. He described how for the first time in his life, he saw the truth "that love is the ultimate and the highest goal to which man can aspire.... I understood how a man who has nothing left in this world still may know bliss, be it only for a brief moment, in the contemplation of his beloved." (Frankl, 2006)

In contrast, without a sense of purpose or moral compass individuals can fall prey to hopelessness and helplessness when faced with pain and loss, putting them at risk for depression, addictions, and even suicide. Finding meaning in one's life is a decidedly human longing. Without it, the realities of aging and death, the loss of loved ones, the stresses of family and of economic problems, can become devastating and insurmountable.

Finding a bigger purpose, a place where we can be of service to other people, animals, or the environment not only gives each of us a reason to persevere but also connects us to communities of like-minded people. We find our "tribe" of people who help us through times of need; we also feel like we matter and have some importance when we can help and give to others.

LEARNING POSITIVE EMOTIONS

The Dali Lama has written extensively about ancient Buddhist teachings that describe the inevitability of suffering and the ways to find happiness. Brain research (Lutz, et. al, 2008) confirms that people become happier when practicing loving thoughts. Functional magnetic resonance imaging (fMRI) was used to determine that positive emotions can be learned in the same way that one learns to play a musical instrument or become proficient in a sport. Emotions and feelings were dramatically changed in subjects who practiced compassionate meditation. Activity increased in the temporal parietal junction of the right hemisphere, an area important to empathy and the perception of the mental and emotional states of others.

Families can improve on this Key by practicing the truths that underlie all the world's great religions, such as the golden rule, forgiveness, compassion, and kindness to others. Embracing religions that focus on intolerance and that are fear-based can actually be a detriment to your health (Newberg and Waldman, 2009). You can make a ritual of volunteering as a family, serving food to the homeless, donating food and clothing to others, reading books, or watching inspiring movies about real life heroes who have faced hardship. For some children, taking care of a pet and learning how to be gentle, loving, and responsible is a powerful early connection. Visit local or distant places where the standard of living is different than your own. It helps children realize that there is more to the world than what is happening in their own backyard. Practicing walking a mile in another's moccasins can go a long way towards building compassion and empathy.

Now that you better understand the nature of this Key, you may want to go back and re-score yourself in the Current Family Assessment.

KEY #8 TIPS: SEEING THE POSITIVE

- Use current events and situations to teach lessons in morality.
- Emphasize learning from mistakes.
- Treat others the way you would like to be treated.
- Practice saying "I'm sorry" at least once a week.
- Volunteer or do community service with your family.
- Emphasize the positive aspects of situations rather than complaining. Practice "letting go."

CHAPTER NINE

KEY # 9
EFFECTIVE PROBLEM-SOLVING

It's not that I'm so smart.
It's just that I stay with problems longer.
-Albert Einstein

*F*amilies make thousands of decisions together and how they accomplish this has a significant impact on the health and happiness of family members. Studies have shown that "problematic" families don't have more problems than families that are doing well... they are just less capable of addressing the problems that they do have (Westley and Epstein, 1969.)

BALANCE BETWEEN AUTHORITY AND INCLUSION

Effective problem solving and decision-making are facilitated by a balance between the principles that we emphasized in Keys #5 and #7. The fifth Key, Who's In Charge, is about parents creating structure and healthy limits appropriate to the age of each child, with parents being in charge. The seventh Key, Accepting Differences, relates to the importance of inclusion and mutual respect among family members, honoring differences and unique perspectives.

In healthy families many decisions can be made in a democratic fashion with everyone having an equal vote, while other decisions are best left to parents alone. In general, families do not work well as democracies. Some decisions are best made in the open, while others should be made behind closed doors. Obviously a different process is in order when deciding financial matters as opposed to where the family chooses to go out to dinner.

When making decisions as a family there is a need for a balance between respect for the feelings and thoughts of each family member, and completing the task at hand. The group needs someone to fill the role of facilitator so that the process doesn't go on forever. Families without such an administrator become frustrated by the lack of organization and direction. On the other hand, in families where decisions are always meted out by an authority figure, family members feel powerless and excluded from the process.

A big advantage of including others in decision-making is that the implementation of those decisions tends to take place with more compliance and less resistance. As children feel heard and included, they are less likely to be oppositional, particularly as they get older. It is also optimal to include the kids' input with as many decisions as are age appropriate. The most challenging but important time to be inclusive with family problem solving is with teens.

Families that do well at making decisions also allow for "healthy disagreement." Family members feel heard and respected for their point of view, even if a decision doesn't go their way. They can agree to disagree rather than feeling pressured to conform. Coming to agreement on a contested issue is one of the best ways that families can foster feelings of mutual respect and self-esteem.

NIP IT IN THE BUD

Problems can be more easily handled when addressed in a timely fashion. Although it's natural to want to deny and ignore certain things, families function best when they are able to identify problems before they become crises. Healthy families try to face their problems when first recognized rather than waiting until things get out of hand.

A frequent complaint that we hear from families after a few sessions is that they feel like they waited too long before seeking help. It is especially common for parents to wish that they had come for help sooner with kids out of control. Although it can take a few weeks to help parents learn to set more effective and caring limits with an aggressive five-year-old, it often takes much longer to help a family with a teen that is out of control.

Stages of Decision-Making

Some persons are very decisive when it comes to avoiding decisions.
-Brendan Francis

A certain amount of leadership and organization is required in order to make effective decisions. There is also a need for follow-through. If you think this sounds like a lot of executive activity, you're right! It takes as many executive skills to run a family as to run a corporation or captain a ship.

A mom, dad, and three teens came in with complaints about not feeling connected to one another. The family's assessment on the 10 Keys was quite good, yet a couple of elements needed attention. The middle son had been escaping the family to be with his friends, but came to tears as he confessed wanting to be better friends with his siblings. The brothers used a few "repair kits" to work out some resentments that had built up, but another challenge was that family members were somewhat passive. Overly cautious, each waited for the other to reach out, which hardly ever happened. Previous family meetings had led to some new resolutions, but there was a lack of leadership and follow through on the decisions they had made. They decided to handle this missing "executive" piece by rotating the leadership role among themselves on a monthly basis.

We find it helpful to offer families the problem-solving stages of the McMaster Model of Family Functioning, as outlined by Epstein, et al. (in Walsh, 2003.) These include:

1. Identification of the problem
2. Communication of the problem to the appropriate person(s)
3. Development of action alternatives
4. Decision on one alternative

5. Action
6. Monitoring the action
7. Evaluation of success

In sum, healthy families face new problems as they come up, make decisions systematically, and follow up to make sure that actions are carried out.

POTENTIAL ROADBLOCKS

Hot heads and cold hearts never solved anything.
-Billy Graham

Perhaps by now it is obvious why the first and second Keys, (Talking and Listening, and Expressing Feelings,) were placed at the beginning of this book. So much comes back to the need for effective conversations and/or dealing with uncomfortable feelings that have gotten in the way. Don't even attempt to solve problems or make decisions when big feelings are clouding things. A good first step is for family members to feel "understood" for their perspective and point of view. Respect and understanding almost magically helps the emotional brain to settle down. Only then can our prefrontal cortex or "thinking brain" effectively engage in problem solving.

Other common barriers to good decision-making are stress and the lack of time or attention. If you wait too long to correct your course, the ship can run aground and cause even more distress. Time to send up the flares… Attending to important decisions early prevents even greater stress.

Finally, the more serious a problem is, the more difficult it can be to face because our defense mechanisms have kicked in. But there is no other real solution than to express and overcome the feelings that are keeping us stuck. Not to decide just doesn't work.

Having strong opinions can also make it difficult to make decisions. As a couple, we used to compromise each time about where we would go out to dinner. Just to be nice we'd find a compromise solution that we would each "tolerate" but neither of us really liked very much. A better solution for us (that we later stumbled upon) was to alternate and have each of our first choices honored every other time rather than to have mediocre compromise solutions each time. -Don and Debra

FAMILY MEETINGS

As family therapists, we have often wondered how many families could have avoided the need for professional help if they had family meetings on a regular basis. Meetings can serve as a time to:

- Make plans and decisions.
- Improve harmony and communications by helping members feel "heard" and respected.
- Practice positive thinking and appreciations of others.
- Resolve conflicts with the use of the "repair kit."
- Schedule fun activities.

TIPS AND TOOLS FOR FAMILY MEETINGS

When you have to make a choice and don't make it, that is in itself a choice.
-William James

Parents may need to play an authoritative role during meetings, but one of the goals of gathering is for family members to express their feelings. You will ideally shift to an attitude of acceptance rather than dominance or control. The rules of the game emphasized in Chapter 5, Who's in Charge, are temporarily suspended in this context. Whether parent or child, when we are immersed in the "feelings world," all family members should be equally acknowledged, valued, and respected for their thoughts and feelings. The use of "I messages" is crucial, as is encouraging everyone to share their thoughts and feelings. When there is good listening, everyone should wind up feeling understood even though they don't necessarily get what they want. (Hightower and Riley, 2002)

Being prepared:

- Before you start, are you as a parent able to provide enough structure and a climate of safety for a meeting?
- Are family members "in control" enough to listen to each other and communicate without blaming or attack? If not, can you provide enough guidance and structure to maintain sufficient harmony anyway?

Getting started:

Let the children know that you will begin holding family meetings to talk about what's going on in everyone's life. If possible, initiate meetings when things are going relatively smoothly. Get the ball rolling when family members *aren't* having lots of negative emotions.

Initial meetings are best focused on the positive rather than diving into heavy issues. With a parent facilitating the process, start by going around the circle and have each person share things that are "new and good." Families with high levels of stress and conflict need this time just to be together in a positive way, perhaps re-learning that being together can be fun and rewarding for a change.

Topics for meetings:

Although a variety of options are possible, we recommend the following topics as a starter package. Don't be discouraged if you can't cover the whole list. Going around the circle, everyone is prompted to:

1. Share something new in their life that they feel good about.
2. Express an appreciation for each family member.
3. Share something that was recently upsetting.
4. Use the "repair kit" and "I messages" to help members work out upsets with each other.
5. Suggest other topics to be discussed.
6. Make decisions for the future, first using a "brainstorming" technique.
7. Discuss schedules of events for the coming week.

8. Set personal and interpersonal goals for each family member, ways to help bring out the best in everyone.

9. End on a positive note, with some fun, food, or frolic!

The Right Timing:

Meetings can be arranged ahead of time or requested at other times by any family member. We recommend that meetings happen initially once a week, but many families like to taper off to meeting every other week. The length of family meetings is largely dependent on the age and attention span of the children. Meetings with two to six-year-olds can last between ten–twenty minutes while those with teens can extend up to an hour if the process is working well. Some families are competing with heavy schedules and do better with regular and prearranged times for meetings. Other families like to be more spontaneous.

Mealtime is not the best choice for a family meeting. Although the positive elements described above can also happen during meals, the skills for successful expression of feelings are best developed without the distraction of food.

The Right Place:

It usually works best to gather in a circle with everyone sitting at the same level, perhaps on the floor with pillows. Convene your meetings in a neutral, fun place at home, and preferably not at the dinner table.

In selecting your spot, you may *not* want to meet in rooms where high conflict has occurred. Meet in a safe new setting that doesn't have a lot of negative associations. Also choose a place that is relatively free of distractions. This is a time for cell phones, computers and TV to be off.

Leading the group:

The job of the group leader for any given meeting is twofold: First, to engage each family member and solicit their input; and second, to keep the process focused and moving so that things don't get bogged down. In the initial phase a parent should manage the meetings to demonstrate the role that an effective leader plays. After a while, as is age appropriate, the kids can take over this role as well.

Other pointers:

■   We recommend that all members of a household, as appropriate, be involved in the family meetings. This can include grandparents, other extended family, nannies, and children who are at least old enough to pay attention.

■   Avoid criticism and show concern for the thoughts and feelings of others through good, attentive listening. Parents should praise and encourage fair treatment as well as coach members not to interrupt.

■   Parents can also model deep breathing as a way to reinforce patience and consideration. If certain family members tend to drone on and on, however, they should be coached to be more concise so as to not lose their audience.

■   If things get "too hot to handle" or out of control, you may want to take a break for fifteen minutes or so and try again. Although some amount of negative "spewing" of feelings can be expected and helpful, sometimes it needs to be curtailed and replaced with some good problem solving.

■   When discussing possible solutions to problems or challenges, use "brainstorming." Each member offers an idea or suggestion without criticism from others. This kind of open forum serves to loosen people's thinking and can add to greater creativity in finding solutions. As you notice the discussion moving off track, you might say, "That sounds like an issue we may want to discuss at another time. If family members interrupt, try, "We really want to hear your opinion, but could you wait until your brother is finished talking?"

■   Try to offer children as much power and influence in the decision-making as they can responsibly handle, but no more. Good topics for group democratic votes are things like where or how to spend weekend, vacation or free time. For larger decisions such as those that have financial implications, parents can have the kids offer their ideas, yet might want to make final decisions behind closed doors.

■   When making group decisions, family members who didn't get their way can practice being a "consenting minority." Example: "Even though I would rather do ____, I will make the best of the situation and have a good time." In this fashion you are teaching an important lesson: how to move beyond self-centered attitudes and go along with the flow of things in a group.

A final key to successful family meetings is to be adaptable and learn from experience. Use what works to help your family ride the ups and downs of family living and to bounce back after stressful events. Families that know how to adapt well tend to have higher levels of family satisfaction. Bear in mind that all families have problems. The crucial thing is to face challenges squarely and early, find new solutions, test them out, and be willing to admit when an idea doesn't work out in practice. This is how we learn and grow.

Now that you better understand the nature of this Key, you may want to go back and re-score yourself in the Family Assessment.

KEY #9 TIPS: MAKING DECISIONS

■   Face problems early rather than waiting until things get out of hand.
■   Provide leadership and organization to make decisions and follow through.
■   Negotiate and compromise rather than one person dominating decision-making.
■   Include children in decision-making in a way that is developmentally appropriate.

- Respect each family member's ideas and feelings.
- Model how to be happy even when you don't get your way.

CHAPTER TEN

KEY # 10
PARENTING TOGETHER

When there is love in a marriage, there is harmony in the home;
when there is harmony in the home,
there is contentment in the community;
when there is contentment in the community,
there is prosperity in the nation;
when there is prosperity in the nation, there is peace in the world.
-Chinese proverb

*W*e spent many hours contemplating just where this Key should go. There was good reason to make it the first Key since the first step in forming a new family is the decision to become a couple, (or in the case of an adult choosing to raise a child on her own, the decision to become a parent). Just as the birth of the child instantly confers the status of parenthood, the decision to partner with another person is one of life's biggest choices. That's where the family begins and that's why the quality of the couple's relationship is so critical to the health and well-being of the whole family. But now that you are reading this chapter, you know that we made the well-considered decision to make this very important Key the final one. For those of you into baseball, think of this Key as the clean-up hitter, the Babe Ruth on whom you depend to hit the big one, the best that's saved for last…

Whether parents are still together or not, the quality of the adult relationship sets the tone and is the basic foundation for the health of the family as a whole. Like it or not, adults provide important models for their children, and to the degree that your model is a positive one, children will relate in a positive fashion. Most parents, ourselves included, sometimes try to get their children to "Do what we say, not what we do." Any benefits from this strategy are likely to be brief and illusory.

So many of our clients come to therapy out of deep concern for their children. We emphasize to parents that the best way to help the kids is not necessarily to get the child their own therapist but to get help for the family. It is far more effective to teach parents the skills outlined in this book so that the family has a blueprint for healthy functioning. If you think about it, what impact could an individual therapist have in one hour of counseling a week that couldn't be unlearned the other 167 hours of the week?

How parents get along is important no matter what family configuration or ethnic community we are talking about—blended families, single-parent households, families headed by gay or lesbian couples, multi-generational families, and foster homes. Just as we are constantly communicating with others through verbal, nonverbal, intentional and unintentional means, we are also modeling how to relate to others every time we interact. Coping skills learned at home are the reason some kids can go through divorces and not be troubled and why others can grow up in two-parent, "married for life" households, and still have serious emotional and behavioral difficulties. The bottom line is that becoming a healthy adult isn't necessarily related to growing up in an intact family. It is the quality of the primary relationships that really matter.

Remember the "Brain Research" at the end of Chapter 2 about the discovery of mirror neurons? By simply watching or hearing others perform an action, certain brain cells in our children light up and mirror our actions as if they were performing the very same behaviors. This "mirroring" is an important mechanism in how children learn to talk as well as how they acquire social and emotional skills. One of the reasons that so many patterns begin in childhood and plague us forevermore, or so it seems, is because of the strength of this learning by imitation. In addition to imitating overt adult behavior, children can also mirror problems that exist within one parent or between the parents.

 A toddler had his day care teachers worried because he was hitting and biting other children. On a closer look at the family, it was obvious that there was an undercurrent of rage between the spouses, although they insisted that they were never angry with each other. The child's acting out disappeared when the parents got help for their relationship and learned how to express angry feelings directly and in a constructive manner. This kind of situation is very common. Children are far more sensitive than we imagine. Long before they can communicate their upsets directly, they may act out or show in behavior the very issues the adults are struggling with but have failed to address.

CHARACTERISTICS OF HEALTHY COUPLES

Women marry men hoping they will change. Men marry women hoping they will not. So each is inevitably disappointed.
-Albert Einstein

Scientific studies have helped us to identify the ten Keys that seem essential to family health. There is also excellent research on the factors that determine success or failure in a marriage. John Gottman and his colleagues in Seattle were featured on the cover of *Newsweek* magazine (Wingart, 1999) with a stunning announcement: being able to predict divorce with over ninety percent accuracy. Thirty-five years of research has led to a lot of practical information and we often prescribe his books to clients needing more depth on this Key.

Gottman's studies suggest that *conflict is intrinsic to and inevitable in all relationships.* What is crucial is how a couple handles conflict. The prevailing myth is that happy couples talk everything out, but Gottman asserts that there are three styles of handling conflict, exemplified by *validators, volatile couples,* and *conflict avoiders.* Validators are couples that talk things out, and when they do, are mutually respectful and capable of compromise and empathy. Volatile couples express both positive and negative emotions with a lot of passion and intensity. Their arguments are more heated, usually louder and more intense. At the other extreme, conflict avoiders rarely fight openly. They do this by downplaying or ignoring complaints and classically agreeing to disagree.

Surprisingly, studies show that there are happily married couples in all three groups (Gottman, 1994). This startling conclusion was out of sync with most therapists' advice, which is to try to get everyone to be validating types (clearly the superior mode, it was thought; and probably still considered a desirable result by many therapists accustomed to success using this model). *What is crucial to happy marriages is the match of styles between the couple and the ratio of 5:1 positive to negative interactions overall.* As long as we find a partner whose preferred mode of fighting is a good match with our own *and* we maintain a positive focus, any of the types can work effectively. *Vive la difference!*

One challenge we encounter as therapists is the mismatch that occurs when a validating type unwittingly marries a volatile type—or even worse, a volatile pairs up with a conflict avoider. In these cases we talk about the research, help the couple to choose which style they are going to settle on, and teach them how to work within the same style while concurrently upping their positive interactions.

It's probably not typical for tattooed Hell's Angels couples to seek therapy, but it happened recently when Maggie and Bart showed up on the front porch of our clinic. A joy to work with because of their sense of humor, they both boasted of being tough and puzzled as to why they each chose to get married for the first time in their forties. Maggie was a no-holds-barred woman who grew up in an Italian family in New York. "Volatile" to the max, she had learned in her childhood to stay protected and "tell it like it is." "So what's Bart's problem that he's upset with me all the time?"

Bart's family was more mellow. He obviously wanted a softer delivery of feelings from his beloved. It's not always this easy, but just five sessions of learning the "repair kit" and practicing constructive ways of dealing with upsets was all that was needed to get them back on the highway of happiness.

RELATIONSHIP KILLERS: CRITICISM, DEFENSIVENESS, CONTEMPT, AND STONEWALLING

Research on couples in the middle of conflict led to the next finding by the Gottman group. If certain behaviors occurred with frequency, these actions were seen as both symptoms of a relationship in distress, and also contributors to more pain. Because of their dire consequences, criticism, defensiveness, contempt, and stonewalling were aptly named "The Four Horsemen of the Apocalypse" (Gottman, 1994). Understand that most couples use these behaviors on an occasional basis, predictably during one of those amygdala hijackings we've discussed. But if all of these behaviors start to become consistent ways of communicating when in conflict, the marriage will likely end in divorce. We use the metaphor that communicating using the Four Horsemen is akin to throwing acid on metal, quickly corroding even the best of relationships.

Most of us launch *criticism* at our loved ones when we are upset. The most damaging form of criticism is accusatory remarks that become global and sound like character assassination. Instead of merely complaining about your spouse arriving home late for dinner you say something like, "You are such an inconsiderate jerk. You are never on time for anything!" Global criticism often breaks the rules taught in Chapter 1 about not using the words "never" and "always" while lodging a complaint.

The second of the horsemen is *defensiveness*, which goes hand in hand with criticism. It is often used when criticism has already taken the stage but is equally corrosive and often followed with a counterattack. A comment illustrating this behavior would sound like, "There's no reason for me to come home on time since *you* never have dinner ready. I'm always on time for things I care about."

The third of the horsemen is *contempt*, which is powerfully destructive. Contempt is criticism turbocharged with extra twists of disgust and disrespect. It is communicated the same way across cultural lines—with eye rolling, scowling, a twisted mouth and sarcastic tone or mocking. Once this weapon has been used, the fourth horseman, *stonewalling*, often emerges. The "stonewaller" withdraws any connection, walking away, withdrawing eye contact, refusing to listen, often with arms folded. For generations it has been called "giving someone the silent treatment."

By the time a typical couple comes for counseling, we witness some or all of the horsemen. Pointing out these behaviors, often exhibited without malice, can help clients to understand why they have been feeling so bad. We make the request that they try to eliminate them from their interactions as much as possible.

Can you identify which horseman is your "personal favorite?" Your answer probably relates to your family of origin. For example, if you had a highly critical parent, you can become defensive as an adult even when no one is criticizing you. Or your family may have seen things in "black and white" instead of being open to different points of view. This may make you inclined to display criticism or contempt when your partner does something you consider wrong.

ANOTHER RELATIONSHIP KILLER: EMOTIONAL DISENGAGEMENT

As you learned in Chapter 4, time and attention are necessary for people to feel close and intimate in relationships. Just as the presence of the four horsemen is an active predictor of divorce, the absence of warmth and a positive connection can be a signal of the impending demise of a relationship. Gottman (1994) found that couples with lots of criticism and contempt were usually divorced within seven years, whereas emotionally disengaged couples tended to break up between seven and fourteen years. These couples often describe their situation by saying, "We simply grew apart." Couples like this can look surprisingly good on the surface since they tend not to fight openly, but on closer inspection show little warmth or interest in one another.

The distancing process, often happening over years, begins initially as a way to avoid a problem. However, suppressing negative feelings takes a toll on both the individual and the couple as they try harder and harder to pretend that everything is okay. If we could make a wish, it would be that couples reach out for help sooner rather than later. This would make our challenges as therapists, and the lives of our clients much easier. The research shows that couples typically come in for therapy an average of six years later than they should. The longer any pattern goes on uninterrupted, the harder to change.

We also caution people who are already in committed relationships to engage in counseling together prior to seeking individual counseling. If your relationship is suffering from emotional disengagement it can be tempting to seek relief alone, but doing so could make things even worse. The best way to solve the problem of an eroding connection is to slowly approach the issues of difficulty and learn to find common ground, move to conflict resolution, and rebuild trust and friendship.

UNSOLVABLE PROBLEMS

What counts in making a happy marriage is not so much how compatible you are, but how you deal with incompatibility.
-Leo Tolstoy

A more recent myth that the Gottman (2000) research dispels is that healthy couples resolve all their problems. Wrong again! It turns out that most if not all couples have a mix of solvable and unsolvable problems. Happy couples handle these categories of problems more effectively. When areas of conflict arise, the couple communicates using tools such as the repair kit. Having heard each other out, they find a tentative solution, often a compromise that they agree to try in the future. Sometimes it takes a few tries but with persistence the process becomes "problem approached, problem solved."

The second class of difficulties, the perpetual or unsolvable ones, often revolve around one person's temperament, cultural or religious differences from their partner, or varied needs such as alone time, sexual contact, or an avid hobby. Once a couple realizes they have an unsolvable difficulty, the idea is to work towards mutual acceptance. Often a good way to do this is to reflect on the parts of you that haven't changed much over the years and how your partner has to tolerate *your* character flaws or needs just as you have to work with theirs.

Happy, loving couples have ongoing conversations about these issues but not from polarized positions where they are trying to change each other. They often gripe about them the way one does about the inevitable aches and pains of aging, but finding a way to empathy, humor, and understanding in spite of frustration or irritation. Trading your partner in for another one (while occasionally very tempting to fantasize about) usually includes swapping one set of perpetual problems for another. That's a pretty practical reason to find creative ways to work with what you've got.

BEING "RIGHT" VERSUS BEING CLOSE

One of the strengths of happy couples is that each partner is willing to yield to the other rather than having to win or be "right." The reason we put "right" in quotations is that, "How do we ever know who is right?" We return to the six blind men and the elephant and the notion that each individual is convinced of knowing what an elephant really is. For almost any topic, all we have is our own point of view. But aren't there indisputable facts? you might ask. Not so, says the research. There is only really "subjective truth." Two different people often give radically different accounts of the same event. And the more that feelings are flying, the more varied our perceptions are. Knowing this, couples that wish to remain close and mutually respectful learn to find a way, when necessary, of simply accepting their partner's point of view.

The essence of this strength is twofold: one part is truly being open to the multiplicity of viewpoints and the complexity of "reality," and the second is being able to concede. Some couples seem to have to bicker over just about anything and everything, turning even the simplest discussion into a debate. What is the fastest way to drive to Grandma's? Which restaurant serves the best tacos? Who started this argument? Even the smallest point can become a big deal if a couple consistently gets into a power struggle.

But what if you "know" you are right and you even have the evidence to prove it? That's all fine and good if you want to be right but create distance with your partner. You can win the battle in the moment, and lose the "war" for a tender, connected relationship. Another way to approach this is to look for the common ground even in the midst of a disagreement.

OFFERING ADVICE TO OUR PARTNER

Most couples struggle with the challenge of giving each other advice. Sometimes the person that you love the most in the world is the last person that you can take input from! One of the reasons this happens is because hearing our partner's voice telling us what we "should" do can instantly trigger feelings of being a child scolded by a parent. The constant refrain is, "I'm so frustrated. I've been telling her that same thing for years, but now when her friend tells her, she listens!"

Here's a simple tool to try with your partner. Instead of offering unsolicited advice, first say "Sweetie, I have some thoughts about the issue we were talking about. Would you like me to share them?" Wait until your partner says yes. If they aren't ready to listen, don't waste your time or words. Make an agreement ahead of time to try this method together. Each of you may be better able to take a deep breath and listen to some good feedback from your beloved.

MAKING UP IS HARD TO DO

Marriage, ultimately, is the practice of becoming passionate friends.
-Harville Hendrix

Happy couples can also remain emotionally connected during or after a disagreement or upset. There are many ways to do this, some of which may look like avoidance but are actually a healthy way to diffuse the negativity that can otherwise build. In addition to apologizing, other ways to rebound are through the use of playfulness and humor, extending a touch or offering a hug, or saying something yielding like, "Let's not fight any more. It's not worth it," or "Let's not let this ruin our whole night."

It's common in every relationship to hurt one another's feelings, step on each other's toes, and annoy one another some of the time. Learn not to sweat the small stuff. Healthy couples don't talk through every slight or interruption but give one another the benefit of the doubt. When your partner tries to metaphorically kiss and make up, consider it an opportunity to practice softening. Find the courage to be the one who reaches out even if the attempt to repair things seems awkward or inept. Very seldom does the same person keep coming forward to say I'm sorry or to make peace if their partner keeps rebuffing moves towards closeness.

THE GIFT OF LISTENING

Ultimately the bond of all companionship, whether in marriage or in friendship, is conversation.
-Oscar Wilde

Another book that we use with couples is *Do I Have to Give Up Me to be Loved By You* by Jordan and Margaret Paul (2002). They outline the difference between listening while still protecting oneself, versus listening in order to learn about your partner. When we are self-protective we get stuck in the power struggle, each trying to convince and change the other. When we listen with an open heart and soft belly, disagreements can become the fountainhead of learning about what makes us tick.

Inspired by the Paul's teachings, we help couples recognize the need for a shift in thinking about the issue of feelings. There is an important reason why individuals feel defensive when their partner is upset with them. The genesis of this reaction is that we were all children once upon a time. Our emotional brains see only the past. As children, if an adult such as a parent or other authority figure was upset with us, there were not so subtle implications that we did something wrong, were in big trouble, and therefore needed to shape up. "They are upset with me, so I need to change" is the legacy that we carry into our couples' relationships as well.

The new model that we teach is "If I am upset, that's my responsibility. If you are upset, that's your responsibility." Instead of feeling defensive as we hear our partner's upsets, like a child being scolded by a parent, the whole paradigm has shifted. We're not in trouble. We aren't being forced to change. In fact, as we help our partner feel understood, give birth to and release their feelings, the air is cleared. Our partner's expression becomes a gift to both of us because we can feel close again. Operating from this model we *want* to seek out and hear our partner's upsets because it's the fastest path back to forgiveness, acceptance, and loving each other again. There's some magic in saying to someone who is upset, "Is that all, or is there more that you want to share?"

CULTIVATING INTIMACY AND FRIENDSHIP

I didn't marry you because you were perfect. I didn't even marry you because I loved you. I married you because you gave me a promise. That promise made up for your faults. And the promise I gave you made up for mine. Two imperfect people got married and it was the promise that made the marriage. And when our children were growing up, it wasn't a house that protected them; and it wasn't our love that protected them—it was that promise.
-Thornton Wilder

It should be obvious by now that awareness and practice of the first nine keys allows a couple to use this tenth Key to unlock the potential of the family. The couple needs to communicate, share feelings, accept differences, and learn to problem-solve together. It might seem silly to reiterate the need to spend time together but this problem surfaces so often in our counseling offices that we choose to risk being repetitive. *The relationship of the couple needs to be one of the highest priorities of the family.* Too much attention to meeting the needs of the children will eventually backfire if the couple doesn't have the glue to keep the marriage working. Hopefully you will spend many happy years together after your children have moved out.

One of our favorite books about marriage is an old classic. Published in 1968 by Don Jackson and William Lederer with a forward by Karl Menninger, *The Mirages of Marriage* exposed some of the commonly held myths about marriage and was one of the early books to explain a systems perspective on marital issues to the general public. It is still worth reading. Couples describing themselves as both stable and happily married revealed the secrets of their happiness. They rarely used the word "love." Instead, the two most important things they mentioned were *mutual respect* and *friendship.*

So many couples come into marriage therapy complaining about their lack of intimacy. The words love and intimacy can be "catchalls" for any of a dozen or so specific issues. We attempt in counseling to focus on specific components or behaviors that make an individual feel intimate and loved. Jackson and Lederer called this the quid pro quo of marriage—a Latin term that means "this for that." Since one person's form of intimacy or way of feeling loved is not necessarily another's, we must negotiate our needs and wants. Each individual is asked to give and to receive the most important things wanted in order to feel close. *Cultivating closeness is an ongoing learning process that takes constant practice and feedback over the course of the life cycle.*

> *Even now as a couple, with thirty-plus years of knowing each other, we discover new things all the time. We will have a misunderstanding, talk about it and learn more about each other's perspective. We will make judgments about what the other has said only to find out that we misinterpreted a look or remark. It makes the relationship more complicated but at the same time more interesting to see how there will always be new idiosyncrasies that we have rarely glimpsed. One of the great lessons that we have learned is to remain open and curious rather than to make assumptions about the way the other is behaving. The old self-help jingle is a good reminder: break up the word "assume" and you make an "ass" out of "u" and "me." –Don and Debra*

We will never be able to do justice to the whole subject of friendship. The most important attributes are developing mutual trust and caring, shared interests and activities, depth of familiarity and understanding, and the tendency to make the most out of positives and not stay centered on the negatives.

Why is it so much easier to give our children unconditional love than to our partner? We often treat our beloved with far less respect than we would a friend. Some of this is normal since we feel safer to "let it all hang out," to be more real and vulnerable with those whom we trust the most deeply. On the other hand, asking ourselves "Would I treat my best friend this way or would I just keep my mouth shut?" can be a good litmus test for whether or not each and every upset needs to be openly communicated to our partner.

FAMILY ALLIANCES

With its own unique structure, every family has unwritten rules that determine the roles each person plays, patterns of closeness and distance between family members, and boundaries that exist between the family and the rest of the world. Members of a family have special alliances or connections with one another, often arising from similarities in interests or temperament. Parents may proclaim that they love all of their children the same, yet feel more closeness with a particular child. If there are three siblings in a family, two of them may be closer to each other than either is to the third sibling. Although natural and normal to have variations like these, families don't do well when there are extreme and consistent patterns of unbalance.

There are many ways to figure out and communicate how close and distant family members are from one another in a given family. A pioneer in the field, Virginia Satir, used to have families stand up in sessions and physically position themselves in her office. We have developed a "Family Alliance Exercise" to help families accomplish this same goal. Try this in a family meeting.

Family Alliance Exercise

Each family member takes a three-by-five card and writes their name on it. Everybody takes a turn arranging the cards on the floor in a way that signifies how close they think each member is to the others. Arranging the cards above or below each other suggests the amount of power each person has. Although okay to disagree, see if everyone can come to a consensus about the placement of the cards.

Now you may want to compare your findings with the following diagram. This one represents a healthy family with a mom, dad and three children. With mom and dad at the top, this arrangement signifies that the parents are in charge in the family, and that mom and dad are at least as "close" to each other as they are to their children. The kids are also close to each other, having their own sibling relationship.

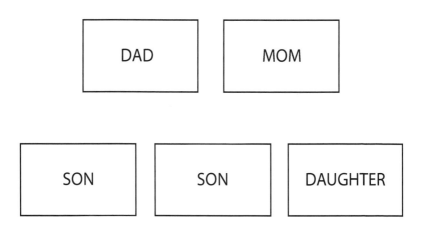

Here's a case example of a family where alliances were problematic:

A family sought help because their teenage son was severely anxious and depressed. In a rather routine initial assessment, family members were asked to explain their patterns of closeness with each other using the "Family Alliance Exercise." It was immediately apparent that mom was much closer to her son than she was to her own husband. The dad also felt closer to his daughter than he did to his wife. Here's how this family arranged the cards:

DAD		MOM
DAUGHTER		SON

As the mom had become so involved and concerned about her son, she had also pulled away from her husband. To the degree that the husband felt left out, the parents polarized into even more extreme positions about what the son needed. As in almost all cases, their lack of connection with one another was both a cause and an effect toward bringing out the worst in their situation. In addition to some good diagnostics and a medication change for the son, some couples work helped things stabilize.

HEALTHY BOUNDARIES

Problems in families can surface when we share too much closeness or secrets with someone from another generation. We just described a case example where parents were closer to their children than they were to each other. It can also be problematic if you, as a parent, are closer to your own parent(s) than you are to your partner.

When two people form a couple's relationship, each partner will ideally feel support for their relationship from their parents, brothers and sisters, and/or grandparents. There is also a need for what we call "healthy boundaries" with relatives. This concept applies to boundaries with friends as well. People outside of our current family can be very important to us, but only in a way that also honors allegiance and connection to the core family itself. The following example highlights this issue.

Jeff and Marcia had a child with a variety of behavioral challenges. After making some progress, Jeff shared his upset with what he described as his wife's overly close relationship with her own mother. In fact, in a symbolic way, Marcia had never really left home. She ran a business with her mom and also spent most of her free time with her. Was Marcia escaping from her marital difficulties by being with her mom, or were her close ties to her mom the reason why her couple's relationship suffered?

We think that it's best to focus our therapeutic work on different hypotheses at the same time. In this particular case, helping this couple get on the same page as parents really meant each of them making a greater effort and commitment to their relationship. When Jeff learned to soften and deal with his anger more constructively, Marcia naturally wanted to spend more time with him. If things hadn't worked out so well, we would have suggested that Marcia's mom be included. Her mom may need support in the future to enhance her life apart from Marcia and to be able to let go, allowing a healthier boundary between generations. Only time will tell.

WHAT ABOUT SEX?

The most important thing a father can do for his children is to love their mother.
-Theodore Hesburgh

In contrast to the prevailing myth, married people, on average, have more sex than single folks. Thirteen percent of married couples report having sex only a few times a year, forty-five percent report a few times a month, thirty-four percent report two to three times a week, and seven percent report four or more times a week (Laumann, Gagnon, Michael, Michaels, 1994).

One of the reasons that couples get married is that they no longer have to hunt for a sexual partner. Although sex is not the "be all and end all" of marriage, intimate relations are a high priority for most couples. Without this physical connection, the relationship can wither.

WHAT LOVE'S GOT TO DO WITH IT

Helen Fisher (1998) has spent years studying the biochemistry of love. Neurotransmitters and hormones such as dopamine, vasopressin, and oxytocin are found to be significant components of bonding and connection. With tender touch and sexual activity, men produce considerable amounts of vasopressin, which lowers stress levels and even improves social skills. Women benefit from a boost of oxytocin that helps them to feel calm, secure, more satisfied with their relationship, and even more productive in life.

Researchers (Bartels and Zeki, 2000) have been able to identify the specific areas of the brain activated by romantic love. Subjects' brains "lit up" differently when shown pictures of their lovers versus their friends. Romantic love stimulates the same neural pathway activated by the same chemical (the neurotransmitter dopamine) as virtually all drugs of abuse. No wonder love can be so addictive, and why some find it impossible to leave even rather painful relationships.

The bedroom is one of the important areas where loving couples work out mutually satisfying agreements. Rarely do two individuals have exactly the same level of desire, the same interest in certain sexual behaviors, the same urges in terms of time of day, forms of fantasy, level of curiosity, or wildness. So, like everything else, finding solutions takes communication, feedback, compromise, and learning to give and receive.

When marital partners each have a low level of interest and desire, they may find other mutually fulfilling ways to feel intimate. But when libidos are mismatched, problems or resentments can develop. When one partner is sexually unfulfilled and the other is unconcerned or has no interest, both intimacy and trust will be damaged. Emotional disengagement will slowly erode the positive connection; eventually infidelity and/or divorce become more likely. Complacency about sex (or any other topic highly important to you or your partner) is a formula for marital unhappiness.

When people come into therapy saying they don't think they *should* have sex if they don't feel like it, we as therapists hear alarm bells. *Withholding love and touch from your spouse is as potentially damaging to the relationship as wanting to look for satisfaction elsewhere.* Unless the couple in question has an agreement about celibacy or open marriage, the complexities of mutual satisfaction ought to be ironed out.

But even when sex is good and frequency sufficient, the marriage can falter. There are, after all, other important areas such as money, parenting styles, shared values, and relationships with friends and in-laws. Any problem left unaddressed can creep into the marriage and bedroom as well. Conflicting sexual needs can be the problem itself and/or the symptom of a growing distance.

As we have shared, there is rarely one cause and one effect in these matters. Problems grow in a circular fashion. A lack of sex can make one partner spend money without communicating. Money problems can create resentment or anxiety that make another person less interested in sex. Rather than diagnosing the person with the lack of sexual interest as the problem, we treat the relationship itself, assessing a couple's strengths and problem areas with the 10 Keys. Couples that emerge from therapy with better skills at communication and the expression of feelings often find that sexual problems disappear.

PARENTING TOGETHER IN DIVORCED FAMILIES

Even though research suggests that children *can* fare quite well when families divorce in a healthy manner (Ahrons, 1995), younger children commonly blame themselves for the circumstances. In one session, a nine-year-old boy screamed, "I hate the divorce and it's all my fault. If I hadn't been so bad, like leaving my spelling book in school, my daddy wouldn't have to hit me with a belt; my mother wouldn't have to yell at him and they wouldn't have to get a divorce."

We have seen countless numbers of kids in therapy who suffer from their parents' splitting up. Out of love for their child, parents often ask for their kids to have counseling so that the child can heal from the break-up of the family. There are times when individual therapy with a child under these conditions can be helpful, but there is no more powerful intervention than a well-orchestrated family session where a child can safely express their feelings to both of their parents… yes, in the same room together.

Often our goal with these kids is to help the parents become capable of good listening and support. Children need reassurance that they are not the source of their parents' problems. One of the first questions we ask kids in a family session is if they know why mom and dad got divorced. To the utter shock of the parents, the kids usually say no or give an explanation that has nothing to do with what happened. Children need to hear a short simple explanation that does not unduly blame one parent. Explanations should focus on the parental conflict: Mommy and Daddy fight too much, or can't agree, or don't live well together.

Children are especially at risk for problems in divorced families with high conflict. One family sought help because the kids kept saying one story to one parent and a different story to the other about how visitations should go. The parents were too angry at each other to meet and talk directly, so they'd call their attorneys and fight in court. The court eventually ordered the children to be seen in family therapy to sort through the maze of confusions. The kids finally confessed to not wanting to hurt either parent's feelings, telling each parent what they thought that parent wanted to hear. Awareness of the pattern helped, but only slightly. The situation improved only after the parents softened and learned to communicate directly with one another.

Kids whose families have split up need to be able to express how they feel about it and ask questions without fear that someone will get mad at them. Once the divorce has occurred they may also need to talk about their struggles with going back and forth between houses. These issues should be revisited throughout the child's dependent years. The feelings and questions will change as the child matures and develops greater understanding of intimate relationships and of the strengths and weaknesses of each parent (which become obvious whether we like it or not.)

Another myth that we try to dispel in therapy is the notion that having another child can fix a marriage that isn't working. Adding a newborn to the family often makes problems more acute. In some stepfamilies the birth of a baby becomes a catalyst for tremendous emotional upheaval. We have witnessed many cases where an older child becomes upset and says she hates the baby, the parent and/or the stepparent. In the case of stepfamilies, to digest that the "new" family is having a baby is to acknowledge, at a deeper level, that mom and dad may not be getting back together again.

There are many excellent resources for stepfamilies. Entire books have been written on this topic alone, and our recommendations can be found in our section on Self-Help Resources. You might also contact the Stepfamily Association at http://www.thestepfamilylife.com

SINGLE PARENT FAMILIES

Single-parent families can also be happy and loving, but it can be lonely, exhausting and difficult to embark on this journey alone. It is essential to find social support. Without personal and social connection there's a strong temptation to wrap your life around your kids. As discussed in Chapter 6, there is such a thing as being too close. Some parents say, "But I don't want to lose the only closeness I have." Although it may feel good to be "friends," the child or teen who takes on the job of being Mom or Dad's protector and playmate also experiences it as a burden. Kids, and especially teens, should be learning how to navigate the world of peer relationships instead of spending too much time with adults.

Single parents often struggle to set limits with their kids. Guilty feelings about a divorce can prevent them from being as firm as they would otherwise be. Although natural to want to overcompensate for the missing parent, it doesn't really help in the long run if critical needs for limits aren't met. Some single parents worry that being too strict will make the kids go live with the other parent.

Since single parents need help and support, particularly if they are working full-time outside the home, they often rely on their parents, siblings or other extended family for help. Putting a child in an environment with multiple authority figures can bring up differences in parenting style between the parent, grandparent or even a babysitter. The necessity of being a team and having team leaders on the same page applies to single parents and whoever is co-parenting with them.

Now that you better understand the nature of this Key, you may want to go back and re-score yourself in the Family Assessment.

KEY #10 TIPS: PARENTING TOGETHER

- Provide children with a model of love, respect, and healthy boundaries.
- Avoid patterns of criticism, defensiveness, contempt, and stonewalling.
- Find agreement as parents and keep conflict away from the children.
- Make your relationship a priority, cultivating friendship and intimacy.
- Yield to the other rather than having to win or be "right."
- Take responsibility for your own feelings, remembering, "If I am upset, that's *my* problem."
- Be as close to your partner as you are to any of your children.

CHAPTER ELEVEN

ECHOES OF THE PAST

I see only the past.
-A Course in Miracles

*T*here are two significant components that contribute to how people get along with one another. The first has to do with the "here and now" factors that we have emphasized with the 10 Keys: the rules, roles, patterns of communication, and means of handling feelings that help bring out the best in everyone.

A second component has to do with the echoes of our past history on present behaviors. If you were one of the lucky people to have been raised in a happy loving family, you've probably emerged with many skills and strengths from your past. However, since most families, even relatively healthy ones, have some bad habits or downright negative patterns, then these too become part of one's legacy. Our histories pack a powerful punch when we've buried old feelings as a way of avoiding the pain associated with them. Unfortunately the "unfinished business" from our childhood and previous relationships also tends to get projected onto and played out with our partner and/or children. It is sad but true that the people we love the most in the world become victims of this process.

Have you ever noticed how you can be a successful mature adult but step into your parent's house and instantly feel like a ten-year-old? Or that a certain movie scene has you suddenly in tears? Or that your father can still scowl at you and make you feel ashamed for existing? Chances are that some part of your past has been evoked in the present moment. And it isn't always pretty…

THE PAST IS IMPOSED ON THE PRESENT

Our "emotional brains" allowed us to survive as a species. We don't have to consciously decide when to approach or avoid certain circumstances. Memories get wired into our brains without our awareness. Events that remind us of an emotionally charged experience from the past can trigger the same feelings associated with that experience (J. Tooby and L. Cosmides, 1990). *The emotional mind reacts to the present as if the past event were happening again.* Furthermore, when we are having strong feelings, the emotional brain can enlist the rational mind to justify that our reactions *are* being created by the present moment, not realizing the influence of the past memory.

This brain science has important implications for how we function. Each of us has what we call "buttons" or "triggers," when old feelings are activated by current circumstances, sights, sounds, or smells. Another example is when emotions flood us as we think about the past. Although getting our buttons pushed can be unpleasant, *we* see this as a good thing because gaining awareness of our unfinished business helps us to resign from being slaves to the past. We playfully challenge clients in therapy, telling them that when they "graduate," one of their final exam questions will be to identify and describe their buttons. We ask, "What unfinished issues, unreasonable expectations, or feelings from your childhood or previous relationships are most likely to leak out and affect your efforts to be a good parent or partner?"

Like items left behind and collecting dust in our office lost and found, here are some examples of buttons you can sort through. Can you claim any of them?

- "I get totally plugged into my childhood and how my dad treated me when my husband starts to raise his voice."
- "I seem to have an anniversary reaction and get really sad at this time of year. I think it's because April is when my parents split up."
- "Trying to be positive with my kids is really hard because

it makes me mad that I didn't receive encouragement as a kid."
- "I felt so smothered by my mom. Now I realize that I push my wife away when she tries to get close to me."
- "I wonder if my chronic anxiety and fears got passed down from the fact that my grandparents just barely escaped from the Holocaust."
- "When my four-year-old daughter says 'No' and gets in my face, it brings up my anger at my dad for spanking me so much.
- "Doc, do you really think I need to be 'right' all the time because that's what my mom did to me?"

If these examples don't grab you, that's okay but it doesn't let you off the hook. We were just trying to stir things up a bit, but everyone is different. If you've got an amygdala, you've got buttons. Maybe you'll just have to plant the seeds of your quest to discover these secrets about yourself and wait to see what surfaces. Or as threatening as it might feel, perhaps you have the courage to ask your partner or children if they have your number.

Without other frames of reference, we also grow up assuming that other families are just like our own. One client asked, "Do you mean that not all dads retreat to the garage every time they feel upset or angry?" Another confessed that he thought that the essence of families is for people to be in conflict all the time. That was his picture of how things were, and therefore how they should be.

Others struggle with the disparity between how their parents treated them as children and how their partner treats them. It is common for men who were spoiled by their moms to expect the same kind of royal treatment from their wives. You can imagine how well this works.

Brothers and sisters are also important influences as to whom we become as adults. One client spent years with a previous therapist focusing on her parents and the neglect and anger she felt from being ignored and mistreated. Very little attention had been paid to the fact that her sister had terrorized her and treated her with contempt. She discovered in therapy that she had also unwittingly "created" a number of friendships throughout her life that mimicked her relationship with her sister. She was all too comfortable in the role of being mistreated. It is uncanny how these ghosts of the past chase us around until we turn around and face them.

FAMILY OF ORIGIN ASSESSMENT

The reason people blame things on previous generations is that there's only one other choice.
-Doug Larson

Now that you've learned the importance of discovering buttons, there will be an additional twist as you complete the **Family of Origin Assessment** for the family of your childhood. This process can help you to learn how your current family patterns may have been affected by past experiences.

For scoring, if you grew up in more than one family for reasons of divorce, a loss in the family, or other reasons feel free to give separate scores for *each*. We have given you a couple of spaces on the assessment form to accommodate additional separate scores. Similarly, if you have difficulty giving your family of origin just one score because things changed so much over time, make some chronological divisions and give separate scores for the different periods of time. (Example: "I really had two distinctly different families. The one while my dad was drinking and the one after he stopped.") Your earliest or more formative years, when you were living at home, are the most important part of our focus.

Turn to the next page and fill out the **Family of Origin Assessment** form. If you have a partner in this process, make copies of the test so you can fill it out independently from one another.

If you prefer, download free copies at **HowsYourFamily.com.**

Family of Origin Assessment

This assessment contains fifty statements, each describing a particular family strength. Looking back, how much improvement do you believe the family of your childhood needed on each item? Grade from 1-5 according to the following scale:

1	2	3	4	5
much need for improvement		some need for improvement		no need for improvement

Family(s) of childhood

Key #1

___ ___ We talked things over and knew what was going on with each other.

___ ___ Individuals spoke for themselves, not for others.

___ ___ Each family member found a balance between talking and listening.

___ ___ We noticed and discussed some of the nonverbal messages we sent and received.

___ ___ We listened to one another's ideas or points of view.

___ ___ Subtotals **Key #1**

Key #2

___ ___ Feelings were expressed in a balanced way, not too much or too little.

___ ___ We comforted one another and were able to cry openly when sad.

___ ___ Feelings of fear, frustration, and anger were shared constructively.

___ ___ As needed, we used calming methods such as centering and slow deep breaths.

___ ___ We shared more positive feelings (joy, tenderness, pleasure) than negative ones (fighting, criticizing, yelling, teasing.)

___ ___ Subtotals **Key #2**

Key #3

___ ___ We recognized and encouraged each other's unique strengths.

___ ___ Mistakes were treated as helpful learning opportunities.

___ ___ We adapted well to losses, changes, and transitions.

___ ___ We practiced good habits of exercise, self-care, and regular sleep.

___ ___ Each of us drew social support from friends, extended family, and social groups.

___ ___ Subtotals **Key #3**

Key #4

___ ___ We liked to spend time together.
___ ___ There were established routines for bedtime, meals, and family time.
___ ___ Family meals together happened more than once a week.
___ ___ We had rituals that were special to our family and/or extended family.
___ ___ Each family member spent some quality time with every other member.

___ ___ Subtotals **Key #4**

Key #5

___ ___ My parents were not too soft but not too strict.
___ ___ My parents were on the same page about how to parent the children.
___ ___ My parents used encouragement and praise far more often than negative words.
___ ___ Punishment consisted of consequences rather than spanking or yelling.
___ ___ The children followed rules and respected the adults as the leaders of the family.

___ ___ Subtotals **Key #5**

Key #6

___ ___ We had a healthy balance between closeness and distance with each other.
___ ___ We felt close and connected to other family members *and* to friends.
___ ___ There was overall respect for each other's needs for independence.
___ ___ Family members were usually available to one another for help and support.
___ ___ We had "boundaries" that provided privacy between adults and children.

___ ___ Subtotals **Key #6**

Key #7

___ ___ Differences among family members were acknowledged and valued.
___ ___ People didn't "need to be right," allowing others to have their own perspective.
___ ___ My parents acknowledged and accepted differences in temperament and learning style.
___ ___ My parents focused on the strengths of individual differences and taught us tolerance.
___ ___ As appropriate, we stated preferences and requests rather than making demands.

___ ___ Subtotals **Key #7**

Key #8

___ ___ We emphasized the positive aspects of situations rather than complaining.

___ ___ My parents taught about social values and moral decision-making.

___ ___ We treated others the way we wanted to be treated.

___ ___ We were capable of offering apologies and being forgiving.

___ ___ We valued spiritual ideas, the bigger picture in life, and service to others.

___ ___ Subtotals **Key #8**

Key #9

___ ___ We negotiated and compromised rather than one person dominating decision-making.

___ ___ We faced problems early on rather than waiting until things got out of hand.

___ ___ My parents were organized and provided leadership in making decisions.

___ ___ Family members felt respected for their ideas even when they didn't get their way.

___ ___ Parents included children in decision-making in an age-appropriate way.

___ ___ Subtotals **Key #9**

Key #10

___ ___ My parents provided a model of love, respect, and healthy boundaries.

___ ___ My parents walked their talk rather than falling back on "Do as I say, not as I do."

___ ___ Criticism and defensiveness happened only infrequently as forms of communication.

___ ___ My parents worked toward agreement and kept conflict away from the children.

___ ___ My parents made their relationship a priority, cultivating friendship and intimacy.

___ ___ Subtotals **Key #10**

___ ___ Total **Keys #1-10**

COMPARING ASSESSMENTS

If you haven't already completed the **Current Family Assessment** or want to revise your answers based upon what you've learned, finish this by returning to the Introduction, pages xi-xiii. In any case, have that test handy so we can proceed with both of the assessments you have completed.

If you haven't already done so, tabulate your scores for your **Current Family Assessment**, circling the Keys that you think might need some attention. Also look at any particular questions for which you scored poorly, even if your overall score for that key was good. (Reminder: If you scored 16–25 points on a Key, see it as an area of strength. If you scored from 12–15, this Key probably needs some attention. If you scored from 5–11, you have identified a significant problem Key.

Following this same process, now tabulate your scores and review your **Family of Origin Assessment.** Notice any similarities or differences between your family of origin and current family. Have any of your buttons been pushed? Does your current family have similar trouble spots or have you left old patterns behind? If you see generational improvement, give yourself a pat on the back. You've probably already done some good work. If not, those keys can become target areas for growth and change.

Now looking more in depth at your family of origin assessment, have you unknowingly overcompensated for past weaknesses? A common example of this is for Key #5, Who's In Charge. Parents who were raised with too much harshness, were spanked a lot, or received little praise, often become too permissive with their own kids. Many people compensate too much and need to come back to a point of greater balance. The following case illustrates an unconscious compensation for another key, Closeness and Distance.

Jean and Harvey brought seven-year-old daughter Sara into our clinic because she was plagued with nighttime fears and couldn't sleep in her own bed. Sara also had separation anxiety during the day, constantly checking to see where her mom was. When Jean completed the Family of Origin Assessment, she realized that she had felt totally abandoned and neglected as a child. Concerned that her daughter would ever feel the same, she had overcompensated as a parent. Her over-involvement not so subtly communicated to Sara that she wasn't safe without constant adult presence. After this realization, Jean became comfortable establishing healthier boundaries and Sara was provided with tools to deal with her fears. This one had a happy ending. The parents were thrilled to reclaim their bed for themselves.

Have you unknowingly replicated the same kind of relationship with your partner that was modeled by your mom and dad? Or conversely, do you find yourself compensating too much for what you saw and didn't want to re-create? These are the important elements to evaluate as you put the magnifying glass to current and past patterns.

Whether you still live at home or not, you may also be curious as to how your brothers, sisters, or parents might evaluate your family of origin. Have there been significant changes in your family over the years? Encourage other family members to complete the **Family of Origin Assessment** and set up a time to compare notes on the phone, if not in person. If you are motivated and willing, it is never too late to make changes in these relationships as well.

CHAPTER TWELVE

MAKING CHANGES

The past must no longer be used as an anvil
for beating out the present and the future.
-Paul-Emile Borduas

*N*ow that you have examined the effects of the past, it's time to come up with a plan of action. This will help you to turn things around and create the family you want. If you are sharing this effort with someone else—your current partner, an ex-partner or any person in a parenting role with your children—it is best to begin as a team. If you are tackling this project by yourself, please adapt the following guidelines accordingly.

STARTING OUT

The first thing to do is to schedule a meeting or series of meetings with your partner. Taking on this assessment requires courage and the ability to admit your shortcomings, so appreciate yourselves. Just as many people refuse to get help when they need it (or even to stop and ask for directions), many choose not to be involved with self-improvement. Be kind to yourself as you move forward. Nobody ever gets a perfect score when it comes to relationships.

Identify Keys with which you are doing well and give yourself a pat on the back. Then take a look at areas needing attention. Review one Key at a time and decide where to start. You may want to focus on your weakest keys or biggest challenges first, particularly if you scored low on Key #1, Talking and Listening, or on Key #2, Expressing Feelings. These Keys are the foundation for all the rest.

Think about the disadvantages of the status quo as well as the potential advantages of change for the better. If you scored poorly on Key #1, you may want to be structured in your first powwow. For example, agree to listen to each other rather than defending your own point of view. The idea is to be gentle with one another. If things between you and your partner are pretty sour, remember that unresolved hurt and/or anger can get in the way of clear thinking and problem solving. Your relationship is the place to start.

SET NEW FAMILY GOALS

A bad habit never disappears miraculously; it's an undo-it-yourself project.
-Abigail Van Buren

Write your goals down on a piece of paper. Just as you might keep a record of which antibiotics work for you, keep track of what you are learning so you can see the big picture as you look back. As things progress over time, learn from both your successes *and* your failures. How did you accomplish positive changes? Are there useful strategies that can be applied to areas that still need attention?

Consider setting goals that can be easily achieved. Examples: Don't start with daily family meals if you have been eating together only once a week. Don't start with a whole list of new chores if the children have never had any. Take small steps; express an appreciation to your partner each evening, spend an hour every other day unplugged from electronic gadgets, put a little note on your dresser that reminds you not to lecture so much. Build on your successes.

If you are motivated, simple solutions might be sufficient to help break old habits and patterns. Given how busy and overwhelmed most of us are, it's easy to forget even the best of intentions. Don't underestimate the value of reminders posted on your refrigerator, computer, or cell phone. A parent who wanted to remember to "catch their child being good" put a three-by-five card on her dresser with a plus sign on it. Another parent placed a rose bud in a vase on the kitchen table. A couple decided to smile more at each other as a reminder to give their child more praise. Be creative and engage your children's imagination and ideas. Anything that feels like a game can make it more fun.

ENGAGE THE CHILDREN IN THE PROCESS

If your kids are old enough and you feel like you're ready, consider having family meetings. (For more input on conducting meetings, see Chapter 9 for a review of prerequisites and guidelines). When even one person changes in a family, chains of reactions can lead to confusion and disruption. Everyone's involvement can make changes happen more quickly because it decreases resistance. Think how much easier it is to diet if everyone stops eating potato chips and ice cream for a while. Consider how you are more likely to start walking every day if someone walks with you.

You are also far more likely to get kids' attention and cooperation if you tell them what *you* are learning or hoping to learn. Become a teaching instead of just a teacher. By admitting the fact that you don't have all the answers you will be modeling the ability to own up to mistakes, be open, honest, and send "I messages" about feelings.

After you have had some successful meetings, follow up to discuss your progress. Is there a way that you can chart improvements from week to week? Many families benefit from counting the frequency of certain target behaviors. Some kids have gotten so involved that they've plotted fun little graphs of changes with different colors, etc. One family had the goal of speaking more respectfully to one another and kept a chart on the refrigerator. Another family decided to have a cussing jar on the kitchen counter. Everyone had to put in a quarter for each swear word they used.

PLAN ON SETTING MORE LIMITS?

The time is always right to do what is right.
-Martin Luther King, Jr.

Bear in mind that many of the changes that you want may not be so exciting for the kids. The most likely example, no surprise, comes when families decide that they have been too permissive and want to set more limits. Give your children advanced warning about the changes you are proposing. (Imagine if the speed limit was suddenly lowered on a familiar road without notice.) If you approach the changes with some enthusiasm and humor, you will also likely get less resistance.

As much as they can participate in a respectful and helpful manner, include the kids in your deliberations about new rules and consequences. It's okay if they don't want to be involved or offer constructive solutions. If that's the case, proceed without them. Remember that even the hint of more rules could inspire a revolt, and things will probably get worse before they get better when you are shifting to new forms of discipline.

We like to use the analogy of surgery. Making big changes in families can be like having your knee operated on. You are taking an action that's bound to be disruptive and temporarily make things worse before they get better. Nevertheless, even though the kids may not like your decision, honor their feelings and the fact that changes can be hard. Finally, know that the eventual result of providing more structure and rules is that your children will be happier and healthier. They'll initially make a stink about the new regime, but everyone benefits when limits are set in a caring fashion. It's a win-win!

Here's one way to explain your intentions to your children:

"In families and life, we all have a job to do. I go to work and my job is to show up, be responsible, do the best I can, and be nice to people. If I don't go to work and decide to hang out in the park instead, I don't get paid. Your job as kids is to have fun, learn new things, do your best at school, and be kind and respectful to others. You receive all kinds of benefits (meals, trips, toys, gadgets) when you do your job, but there will also be consequences when you are not being respectful, helpful, kind, or following rules. My job here at home is to be take care of you and help you to learn these things."

ROADBLOCKS TO CHANGE

Whether you think you can or you think you can't, you are right.
-Henry Ford

We want to share another little secret about people's "mixed motivations" toward positive change. Most people consciously want to be successful, happy, and close to others, but are simultaneously influenced by unconscious forces of resistance. Clearly something very powerful gets in the way. When you think about it, if changing bad habits were easy there wouldn't be as many hot-tempered, cigarette-smoking or constantly tardy folks around.

Often what can sabotage our desire to change is the fear of what might happen next. In one example in Chapter 6, we talked about the importance of recognizing and addressing fears of closeness. The following case example illustrates another kind of unconscious roadblock.

> A single parent mom was unable to follow through on suggestions offered about parenting her teen. She agreed with the recommendations but just couldn't pull them off. This mom was extremely capable and successful in every other aspect of her life. In desperation after weeks of failure, we asked her to do some homework, writing a list of "Some of the top-ten silly, subtle, and/or stupid reasons why you don't deserve to be happy and successful." She opened our session two weeks later in tears, realizing she had been failing because she felt guilty. "How can I let myself be successful and happy when my sister, whom I love so dearly, has been suffering in a mental hospital since she was sixteen years old?"

We call these underlying unconscious roadblocks "silly, subtle, and stupid" because they aren't rational or make sense—things like the illusion that our suffering helps another, feeling responsible for our parent's divorce, guilt over stealing a candy bar at age ten, not being able to fix our alcoholic parent, and so on. Although judging ourselves harshly about them, we wouldn't blame or judge others for that same thing! Though we may not be aware of them, these subtle saboteurs can be steering us in the wrong direction.

Take the challenge.

Set aside time to create your own list of silly, subtle, and stupid reasons why you feel like you don't deserve to be happy and successful. It's time to let all that stuff go.

FINAL PERSPECTIVES

If you change the way you look at things, the things you look at change.
-Dr. Wayne Dyer

In our experience, there are rarely single or simple explanations for family problems. Examples: "My son is acting like this because he was adopted," or "Everything would be okay if she'd just be nice to his sister." In our sharing of case examples throughout this book we may have highlighted certain single themes to make a point, but most family problems, especially when they persist, have a combination of factors in play.

As an example, siblings fighting all the time could be due to the parents not being on the same page, to the lack of rituals and routines, to the temperament of one of the kids, to the sleep deprivation of everyone involved, to being teased at school, to all of the above or to ten factors not yet covered. Using the lens of the 10 Keys is like having a pre-flight checklist. The pilot can't take off until all of the necessary tasks are completed and checked. Similarly, deep and lasting change in a family is not likely to happen until these critical factors are addressed.

If you are a parent of a difficult child, pay attention to his or her biological challenges and temperamental uniqueness. Provide your child with care and services that can address their needs as individuals, but *also* learn and practice the methods of communication, expression of feelings, respect for boundaries, setting of limits, and the other tools that we have described. Don't keep repeating what hasn't worked. Your attempted solutions may even be making things worse. Try something different.

Another way to gain perspective is to connect with others who are in the same boat. There *are* times in the family life cycle that are more difficult. There *are* certain kids, through no fault of their own, who are challenging to raise. If you are the parent of an infant that is not sleeping and is colicky during the day, the whole family can feel it. If your partner is out of work for months or suffering from chronic pain, the whole family will feel the impact. This will be true whether or not you are implementing the 10 Keys. In order to get through these painful passages, remind yourself that you are not crazy, get support from friends and family, and find little ways to take care of yourself in the meantime.

ADDITIONAL HELP

Although we would hope that this book has "solved all the problems in the world," perhaps you've decided that you need to extend your search. We have compiled an annotated list of books in our section on Self-Help Resources. Listed by Key, these select recommendations are the result of years of reading, prescribing books to clients, and receiving feedback about each book's content and value.

If your efforts to achieve the desired changes in your family fall short, it may be time to seek professional help. Most of us have the spirit of the Western cowboy or pioneer in us. We want to do things on our own, especially in relation to family or "personal" matters. Even when we're courageous enough to admit to having problems, we should be able to work things out on our own. This "myth" of hard-nosed independence can be a tremendous asset; it can also be a detriment to our children's and our own best interests when good therapy might help.

Remember that the best time to seek therapy is *before* small problems become big ones. This can save a lot of time, money, and anguish in the long run. People often underestimate the seriousness of their situation and wait until everyday difficulties become crises. We encourage families to get "check-ups" for preventative mental health, especially if they have a question or discomfort about how someone in the family is doing. For your convenience, we have posted additional information about seeking a therapist on our website.

CONCLUSION

Attitude is a little thing that makes a big difference.
-Winston Churchill

We hope that by reading this book you have expanded your sense of who you are and have learned how intricately and intimately connected you are to your family and loved ones. We encourage you to set some new goals for enhancing the quality of your relationships and to implement some concrete changes as you move forward. Each of us gets to choose whether to be bound by past influences or not, between responding reactively whenever our buttons get pushed or crafting a new future for our family and ourselves.

It may take a lot of support to unlearn old habits and it will certainly take time. Do you know other parents who have made positive changes with the same struggles? Most people who have the good fortune to live in healthy families have created them through hard work. Discuss with them how they accomplished a healthier way of being, and look for ways that you can be mentored in this journey.

Here are some of the most important things that we, the authors, constantly remind ourselves in order to remain happy and loving with each other and with our kids. This list isn't really on the 'fridge, but on the metaphorical refrigerator of our minds. We'll let you take a peak...

- Move beyond blame when things go wrong. The person to change is you.
- Take responsibility and empty your emotional "garbage" on your own.
- Challenge negative thinking and celebrate each moment.
- Give up the need to be right. Better to feel close and loving.
- Choose to be happy no matter what.
- The best gift you give your kids is to tend your own garden.

Improving your family and learning to become more loving is best seen as a form of spiritual practice, intended to make us kinder, gentler, better human beings. It is a goal to be lived day by day rather than crossed at a finish line. As anyone who has adopted meditation, yoga, or prayer will attest, even the most adept teachers continue to practice for the course of their lifetime. The same is true for athletes who want to stay in shape, artists who create beautiful paintings, and musicians playing instruments. And when practice becomes habit, life becomes easier because less effort is involved.

No one would imagine that one day they'd wake up and never need to practice again. Yet somehow, when it comes to relationships, we think we should "know by now." The truth is that the best we can be is a work in progress—a precious, one of a kind, ever-growing work in progress. We all have work to do, and we are in it together. Given the magnitude of the changes facing our world and our children, we need each other more than ever. What better gift to ourselves, to our children and our children's children than to build the skills and mindset of a happy loving family.

Blog
Video Blogs
Frequently Asked Questions
Downloads of "Family Assessment Forms"
"Clinicians' Corner"

Available on our website at
HowsYourFamily.com

THE SEED

It seems so many days now
since I patted the egg, gingerly,
into the ground.
I've had to learn
about waiting.
I close my eyes
and search within the moist darkness
to watch the struggle:
Reaching, stretching upwards,
the slender fingers point.
At last
there is only a shell to crack:
rock covered, rigid earth;
I hear the sharp snap,
the cry of pain, feel the first glare of light his hungry eyes.
I opened mine,
fancy a glimpse of green.

The next day
two tiny leaves
like praying hands.

- Debra

Key #1- Talking and Listening

Messages: The Communication Skills Book by Matthew McKay. 2009. Includes active listening, reading body language, developing conflict resolution skills, talking to children, communicating with family members, public speaking, and handling group interactions.

The Messages Workbook: Powerful Strategies for Effective Communication at Work and Home by Davis, Paleg, and Fanning. 2004. This workbook helps you apply communication skills with worksheets, fill-in exercises, and case stories. Includes how to communicate with teens and children.

How to Talk So Kids Will Listen and How to Listen So Kids Will Talk by Adele Faber and Elaine Mazlish. 1980. This book is still in print because it is a classic. It helps parents acknowledge kids' feelings while still being in charge, how to treat others with respect and also giving praise and recognition.

The Wisdom of Listening by Mark Brady, Editor. 2003. A beautiful anthology of spiritual contributions on the art of listening by teachers from varied disciplines, including hospice workers, Ram Dass, Joan Halifax on council circle, Almaas on the Diamond Heart approach, Marshall Rosenburg on Nonviolent Communication, etc.

People Skills: How to Assert Yourself, Listen to Others, and Resolve Conflicts by R. Bolton. 1986. A communication-skills handbook that includes skills around listening, assertion, conflict resolution, and collaborative problem solving, with each building upon the others.

Nonviolent Communication: A Language of Compassion by Marshall Rosenberg. 2003. Guidelines to express yourself and listen to others by focusing your consciousness on four areas: what you are observing, feeling, needing, and requesting to enrich your life. These skills foster deep listening, respect, and empathy, and engender a mutual desire to give from the heart.

Why Don't We Listen Better? Communicating & Connecting in Relationships by J. Petersen. 2007. Concrete strategies to improve communication skills through Talker/Listener cards, especially for tough conversations.

Key #2- Expressing Feelings

Emotional Intelligence: Why It Can Matter More than IQ by Daniel Goleman. 2006. This classic book is the first to explain the importance of emotional intelligence. Goleman argues that our emotions play a much greater role in thought, decision-making, and individual success than is commonly acknowledged. Emotional intelligence is defined as a set of skills, including control of one's impulses, self-motivation, empathy, and social competence in interpersonal relationships.

Social Intelligence: The New Science of Human Relationships by Daniel Goleman. 2007. In this companion volume to *Emotional Intelligence*, Goleman draws from research in the emerging field of social neuroscience. Despite the different title, he covers new research on the topic of emotions as well. Describing what happens to our brains when we connect with others, he explains how relationships have the power to mold not only human experience but also human biology. From a neurobiological perspective he describes sexual attraction, marriage, parenting, and much more.

The Healing Power of Emotion: Affective Neuroscience, Development & Clinical Practice by Fosha, Siegel and Soloman. 2009. A dialogue among eminent neuroscientists, clinicians, attachment researchers, and body workers, drawing on cutting-edge neuroscience to better understand emotion. Explains how emotions can become powerful catalysts for the transformations that are at the heart of the healing process. Both positive and negative emotions are examined from research and clinical observations. The role of emotion in bodily regulation, dyadic connection, marital communication, play, well-being, health, creativity, and social engagement is explored.

Raising An Emotionally Intelligent Child: The Heart of Parenting by Gottman, Declaire, and Goleman. 1998. Helps parents assess their parenting styles and levels of emotional self-awareness. Teaches a five-step "emotion coaching" process to help children recognize and address their feelings; recognizing that dealing with emotions is an opportunity for intimacy; listening with empathy; setting limits; and problem-solving.

More on dealing with anger:

The Dance of Anger: A Woman's Guide to Changing the Patterns of Intimate Relationships by Harriet Lerner. 1985. An excellent book about women who often handle anger indirectly rather than openly. Discusses the usefulness of anger in intimate relationships and healthy ways to express it.

The Anger Workbook by Lorrainne Bilodeau. 1994. Exercises and insights for healthier anger management. Begins with investigating your attitudes about anger with a checklist, explains the role of anger and how it works biochemically, and details the use of constructive anger.

The Dark Side of Love: The Positive Role of Negative Feelings by J. Goldberg. 1999. A convincing argument that hate is the counterpart to love and will always surface in intimate relationships. If not denied, it can be used as a constructive force.

When Anger Hurts: Quieting the Storm Within by McKay, Rogers and McKay. 2003. An excellent resource for parents using yelling, put-downs, and anger in their discipline. Draws on research about anger, including chapters on emergency anger control, the interpersonal and physiological costs of anger, and road rage. Includes techniques for creating an anger-coping plan and anger inoculation.

More on help for mood states:

The Anxiety and Phobia Workbook by E. Bourne. 2005. An award-winning workbook with step-by-step directions for relaxation training, assertiveness, elimination of negative self-talk, changing mistaken beliefs, coping with panic attacks.

Mind Over Mood: Change How You Feel by Changing the Way You Think by Greenberger and Padesky.1995. Offers deceptively simple but powerful and sophisticated strategies for coping with depressed and anxious moods and interpersonal difficulties. Researched based step-by-step instructions and tools.

Feeling Good: The New Mood Therapy by David Burns. 2000. An excellent best-seller that teaches effective cognitive-behavioral methods to free yourself from anxiety, guilt, pessimism, procrastination, low self-esteem, and other "black holes" of depression without drugs.

Key #3- Adapting to Change

On resilience:

Raising Resilient Children: Fostering Strength, Hope, and Optimism in Your Child by Robert Brooks and Sam Goldstein. 2002. A practical handbook with a treasury of suggestions for nurturing a child's strengths and self-esteem. The authors also have a number of other books on this topic, such as *The Power of Resilience.*

Spark: The Revolutionary New Science of Exercise and the Brain by John Ratey and Eric Hagerman. 2008. Filled with case studies, the authors comprehensively explore the connection between exercise and the brain. Exercise can help with symptoms of depression, anxiety, ADD, addiction, aggression, menopause, etc.

The Promise of Sleep by W. C. Dement and Christopher Vaughan. 2000. Covers topics like sleep debt, biological clock, circadian rhythm, insomnia, sleep apnea, narcolepsy, and why we need sleep and dreams. Learn to assess your personal sleep situation, measure sleep debt, evaluate risk of sleep disorders and adopt a "sleep-smart lifestyle."

On dealing with loss:

How to Survive the Loss of a Love by Melba Colgrove, Harold Bloomfield, and Peter McWilliams. 1991. A short and sweet little book with a hundred suggestions about taking care of oneself while in the grieving process.

The Grief Recovery Handbook by J. James and R. Friedman. 2009. A step-by-step program with very helpful exercises for moving beyond loss.

Necessary Losses by Judith Viorst. 1986. Beautifully written book that addresses how loss is an inevitable part of life and helps us become more human. Learn how to release feelings about losses and how they can help us to develop a positive identity and self-image.

On Death and Dying by Elizabeth Kubler-Ross. 1970. Dr. Ross introduced the now-famous five stages of dealing with death: denial, anger, bargaining, depression, and acceptance. Helps normalize the process of grieving and all the stages before bereavement is completed.

Who Dies?: An Investigation of Conscious Living and Conscious Dying by Stephen Levine and Ondrea Levine. 1989. A combination of Eastern and Western spiritual perspectives to help those anticipating their own or someone else's death.

Helping Children Grieve: When Someone They Love Dies by Theresa Huntle. 2002. This straightforward book helps adults talk to children during a time of crisis. Explains common reactions (emotional, physical, and behavioral) parents can expect from children of all ages, and offers adults tools to help children cope with a significant loss.

Key #4- Sharing Time Together

The Book of New Family Traditions: How to Create Great Rituals for Holidays and Everydays by Meg Cox. 2003. Fresh ways of commemorating holidays and creating observances for birthdays, bedtime, dinnertime, and a host of unexpected traditions: sports rituals, pet rituals, homework rituals, vacation rituals, and family meetings, etc.

The Art of Family: Rituals, Imagination, and Everyday Spirituality by Gina Bria. 1998. A book to help create a personal family culture around the domestic rituals associated with family, assigning special meaning to the everyday tasks that make up home life.

Simplicity Parenting: Using the Extraordinary Power of Less to Raise Calmer, Happier, and More Secure Kids by Kim Payne and Lisa Ross. 2010. Covers four levels of simplification: environment, rhythm, schedules, and filtering out the adult world. Parents can tackle extraneous stimulation by simplifying, limiting scheduled activities, providing valuable downtime, storytelling, and periods of quiet.

Key #5- Who's in Charge?

General parenting books:

Emotionally Intelligent Parenting by Maurice Elias, et al. 2000. This excellent book picks up where Daniel Goleman's *Emotional Intelligence* leaves off, translating basic principles into specific parenting tactics for solving daily family issues. Includes exercises for raising the family "humor quotient," becoming aware of feelings, praising and prioritizing, and coaching children toward responsible action.

Between Parent and Child by Haim Ginott, Alice Ginott, and H. Wallace Goddard. 2003. This revised edition of the 1965 classic is an excellent parenting text on the use of discipline without threats, bribes, sarcasm, and punishment. Teaches how to praise without judging, express anger without hurting, and acknowledge children's points of view.

How to Handle a Hard-to-Handle Kid: A Parent's Guide to Understanding and Changing Problem Behaviors by C. Drew Edwards. 1999. Explains why some children are especially aggressive and disruptive. Understanding is key to helping kids become responsible, competent, and content. Emphasizes support with structure, blending positive and negative feedback, including children in the discipline process, and guiding them toward greater responsibility.

Children: The Challenge by Rudolph Dreikurs and Vicki Soltz. 1964. Raising happier, better-behaved children with a program that teaches parents to deal with common childhood problems from toddler through preteen years.

Parenting by Heart: How to Stay Connected to Your Child in a Disconnected World by Ron Taffel and Melinda Blau. 2002. Based upon a series of parenting workshops, this book aims to debunk the most common, damaging myths of parenthood and replace them with flexible solutions.

Parenting Toddlers:

Toddler Taming: A Survival Guide for Parents by Christopher Green. 1985. Excellent, humorously written book that teaches use of timeout and other appropriate strategies for parents of young children. Includes toilet training, tantrums, sleep problems, fidgeting, and special advice for working mothers and single parents.

1-2-3 Magic: Effective Discipline for Children 2-12 by Thomas Phelan. 2010. Describes a system of discipline using counting and timeouts. Good advice on how to parent unemotionally with a lot of common sense, concrete examples, and humor.

Parenting Tweeners:

The Big Book of Parenting Solutions: 101 Answers to Your Everyday Challenges and Wildest Worries by Michele Borba. 2009. Ways to deal with difficult issues such as biting, temper tantrums, cheating, bad friends, inappropriate clothing, sex, drugs, peer pressure, and much more. Written for parents of kids ages three–thirteen, this book helps readers identify underlying reasons for behaviors or problems, and work with ten essential principles of change.

Parenting Teens:

Childhood Unbound: Saving Our Kids' Best Selves—Confident Parenting in a World of Change by Ron Taffel. 2009. Helps us understand our sons and daughters from an entirely new perspective: as a distinctive "free-est" generation, born to "post-baby boomer" parents, subjected to enormous cultural change. Kids now act entitled, use back talk, negotiate endlessly, worship celebrity, do ten things at once, conduct independent lives online, and engage in high-risk behavior at younger ages. At the same time, they are more open with their parents and empathetic. Raising kids during the blossoming of the "Virtual Age."

Uncommon Sense for Parents With Teenagers by Michael Riera. 2004. The author is a high school counselor with great advice for parents that sometimes goes against established ideas: don't give advice even when asked, embrace estrangement (it's part of your teenager's development), and take a demotion and move from "manager" to "consultant."

The Good Enough Teen: Raising Adolescents with Love and Acceptance by Brad Sachs. 2005. A developmental overview of what parents can expect from their children during adolescence. Delineates five stages in the journey towards accepting a child for who he or she is. Includes prescriptive tools and strategies for parents, including checklists, quizzes, and exercises.

Key #6- Balancing Closeness and Distance

Gift from the Sea by Anne Morrow Lindbergh. 1997. A beautiful book of essays about marriage written by a woman in midlife. Poetic metaphors help normalize the ebbs and flows of closeness, distance, self, and other.

Dancing in the Dark: The Shadow Side of Intimate Relationships by Douglas and Naomi Moseley. 1993. A good explanation of how parent/child roles get reenacted in marital relationships and get in the way of intimacy.

The Fragile Bond by Gus Napier. 2010. Translates family system ideas into layman's terms (e.g. how family of origin issues get replayed relationship with our partner and children, etc.) An excellent book for men struggling with issues of equality with a partner.

Key #7- Accepting Differences

A Mind at a Time by Mel Levine. 2003. Incorporates research to show how eight neuro-developmental systems evolve, interact, and contribute to a child's success in school. Instructs how to teach directly to a child's strengths.

An Adult Child's Guide to What's Normal by John and Linda Friel. 1990. For people who grew up in dysfunctional families and need some guideposts. Fits with twelve-step programs and includes issues such as perfectionism, boundaries, co-dependency, cognitive interventions, and affirmations.

The Good Enough Child: How to Have an Imperfect Family and Be Perfectly Satisfied by Brad Sachs. 2001. Helps parents accept their child's limitations while truly seeing, appreciating, and nurturing the child they were given. Sachs points out that we have become a clan of overly anxious mothers and fathers who place far too much pressure on our children as well as ourselves.

Parenting From the Inside Out by Dan Siegel and Mary Hartzell. 2004. This book explores the extent to which our childhood experiences shape the way we parent. Drawing upon stunning new findings in neurobiology and attachment research, they explain how relationships directly impact the development of the brain.

Now That You Know...What Every Parent Should Know About Homosexuality by Betty Fairchild and Nancy Hayward. 1989. Excellent for promoting greater awareness and understanding. Empathetic to the perspectives of parents as well as gay sons or daughters.

Understanding Your Child's Temperament by William Carey. 1999. Profiles children's temperament according to nine aspects: activity, adaptability, distractibility, initial reaction, intensity, mood, persistence and attention span, regularity, and sensitivity.

You Just Don't Understand: Women and Men in Conversation by Deborah Tannen. 1990. Describes how communication styles either facilitate or hinder personal interactions. Men and women are essentially products of different cultures, possessing different but equally valid communication styles.

Key #8- Seeing the Positive

Learned Optimism: How to Change Your Mind and Your Life by Martin Seligman. 2006. Pessimists believe that bad events are their fault, will last a long time, and undermine everything. Optimists believe that defeat is a temporary setback or a challenge—it doesn't knock them down. Pessimism can be overcome with cognitive skills that enable you to take charge, resist depression, and make you feel better.

How God Changes Your Brain by Andrew Newberg and Mark Waldman. 2009. An excellent guide on the interface between spirituality and neuroscience, and means of enhancing our emotional and physical well-being.

Ancient Wisdom, Modern World: Ethics for the New Millennium by Dalai Lama. 2001. A spiritual handbook that provides prescriptions for spiritual expansion, techniques of contemplation, and attitudes to approach environmental challenges.

Wherever You Go, There You Are by Jon Kabat-Zinn. 2005. An excellent book that translates concepts from Zen Buddhism into easily accessible practices.

Chicken Soup for the Soul: All in the Family: 101 Incredible Stories about our Funny, Quirky, Lovable & "Dysfunctional" Families by Jack Canfield, et.al. 2009. Filled with heart and humor, a collection of wacky as well as more poignant stories that highlight the wonderful delights and challenges of being in families.

Live Inside Out, Not Upside Down by Fran Lotery and Sherry Melchiorre. 1996. An excellent resource to help people reconnect to their true selves through a centering process. Readers learn to use their own inner strength and wisdom to resolve life difficulties, make decisions and create a calm and relaxed state of consciousness. Companion workbook and audiotape also available.

Grist for the Mill by Ram Dass and Stephen Levine. 1995. With lots of personal sharing, this book talks about how to see the difficult things in life as "grist for the mill," or vehicles to become more spiritually aware.

You Can't Afford the Luxury of a Negative Thought by Peter McWilliams and John-Roger. 1991. An upbeat, accessible book about the power of positive thought. Negative thinking is seen as a debilitating habit that will slowly kill your spirit—and even lead to physical illness.

The Road Less Traveled by M. Scott Peck. 2003. A classic book that describes a psychology of love, traditional values and spiritual growth. The happiness of your partner is valued as highly as your own.

A Course in Miracles, by Helen Shucman, 2007. An extremely profound and useful self-study program of spiritual psychotherapy. The Course emphasizes that it is but one version of the universal spiritual curriculum, and includes daily lessons in the Workbook for Students. There are many other paths that all lead to God in the end.

The Gift of Change, by Marianne Williamsen. 2006. An excellent description of principles from *A Course in Miracles.* Her primary message is that we not submit to our egos, which tell us we are separate from God, but surrender to God, of whom we are all a part.

Key #9- Effective Problem Solving

Our Family Meeting Book: Fun and Easy Ways to Manage Time, Build Communication, and Share Responsibility Week by Week by Elaine Hightower and Betsy Riley. 2002. This excellent book helps families manage their time and priorities through short, weekly family meetings.

Parent Effectiveness Training: The Tested New Way to Raise Responsible Children by Thomas Gordon. 1975. Describes one of the first national parent-training programs to teach parents how to communicate more effectively with kids. Step-by-step advice to resolving family conflicts so everybody wins.

Key #10- Parenting Together

The Dance of Intimacy: A Woman's Guide to Courageous Acts of Change in Key Relationships by Harriet Lerner. 1989. Written primarily for women but equally applicable to men. Teaches how to move beyond blame and projection and to increase self-focus. Good for ideas for intimate relationships with healthy boundaries rather than codependency.

Getting the Love You Want by Harville Hendrix. 1988. An excellent resource that shows how patterns of relating learned in childhood become unconsciously transferred to our partner. Includes specific techniques and exercises to help couples get closer and reduce projection.

Do I Have to Give Up Me to Be Loved by You by Jordan Paul and Margaret Paul. 2002. A bestseller and one of our favorites about taking responsibility for our own feelings. Describes control patterns, whether subtle or direct, that sabotage communication, and prescribes exercises and techniques that couples can practice together.

Why Marriages Succeed or Fail: And How You Can Make Yours Last by John Gottman. 1995. Written by a psychologist who has spent twenty-five years studying what makes marriages last. Excellent methods to evaluate, strengthen, and maintain a long-term relationship. Includes a series of self-tests (e.g. on style of conflict) to help determine what kind of marriage you have, where your strengths and weaknesses are, including the "Four Horsemen").

The Seven Principles for Making Marriage Work by John M. Gottman. 2000. Most relationship books assert that the key to a solid marriage is communication, communication, communication. "Phooey," says Gottman. There's much more to a good marriage than sharing every feeling and thought. Debunks many myths about divorce: the idea that affairs are at the root of most split-ups, that couples need to resolve every problem, and that occasional screaming matches are necessarily destructive.

On sexuality:

Hot Monogamy: Essential Steps to More Passionate, Intimate Lovemaking by Pat Love. 1995. Includes a nine-step program that starts with a self-quiz for each partner to determine "sexual style." Common problematic issues are communication and resolving differences in desire. Also includes a useful chapter on variety and experimentation.

Passionate Marriage: Keeping Love and Intimacy Alive in Committed Relationships by David Schnarch. 2009. Asserts that men are more likely to let a relationship suffer in order to hold on to a sense of self, while women are more apt to let their identity suffer to help strengthen it. Explicit tips on how to alter this pattern, and why compromise isn't always the best route to take when conflicts arise. Teaches how to deal with uneven sexual desire and initiation, battles about sex, self-image problems, and trust issues.

Mating in Captivity: Unlocking Erotic Intelligence by Esther Perel. 2007. Recommends innovative strategies for rekindling eroticism: cultivating separateness (e.g., autonomy) in a relationship rather than closeness (entrapment); exploring dynamics of power and control; and learning to surrender to a "sexual ruthlessness" that liberates us from shame and guilt. Encourages fantasy and play and offers the estranged modern couple a unique richness of experience.

Divorce and stepfamilies:

Mom's House, Dad's House: Making Two Homes for Your Child by Isolina Ricci. 1997. This classic book guides separated, divorced, and remarried parents through the hassles and confusions of setting up a strong, working relationship with the ex-spouse in order to make two loving homes for the kids.

The Good Divorce by Connie Ahrons. 1995. Ahrons' longitudinal study of post-divorce families offers hope that spouses splitting up may be able to handle their breakup in a way that will permit both adults and children to emerge as emotionally healthy as they were before the divorce. Steps to make a "good divorce" more likely.

How to Win as a Stepfamily by Emily and John Visher. 1991. An excellent book that guides readers towards forming remarried families, considering such issues as former spouses, new grandparents, and legal issues involving custody, visitation, adoption, and financial arrangements.

Families Apart by Melinda Blau. 1995. Offers ten commandments of co-parenting: heal yourself, act maturely, listen to your children, respect your ex as a parent, divide parenting time, acknowledge your differences, communicate, step out of gender roles, recognize and accept change, and know that co-parenting "is forever."

Helping Children Cope with Divorce by Edward Teyber. 2001. Describes the stress and pain children experience and explains how best to shield them from the parents' own conflicts. Guidelines for cooperative child rearing, how to explain the divorce to children, and deal with kids' feelings of responsibility and reunification fantasies.

BIBLIOGRAPHY

Ahrons, Constance. 1994. *The Good Divorce: Keeping Your Family Together When Your Marriage Comes Apart.* New York: Harper Collins.

Ainsworth, Mary, et al. 1979. *Patterns of Attachment: A Psychological Study of the Strange Situation.* London: Psychology Press.

America's Children: Key National Indicators of Well-Being. 2010. (Accessed January 2011) http://childstats.gov/americaschildren/index.asp

American Academy of Pediatrics. 2001. "Children, Adolescents and Television," *Pediatrics*, 107 (2) 423–26.

Anderson, C., D. Keltner, and O. John. 2003. "Emotional convergence between people over time," *J. of Pers. and Soc. Psych.*, 84: 1054–68.

Bahr, S. and J. Hoffman. 2010. "Parenting style, religiosity, peers, and adolescent heavy drinking". *J. Stud. Alcohol Drugs* 71 (4), 539–43.

Bartels, A. and S. Zeki. 2000. "The neural basis of romantic love," *Neuroreport.* Vol 11: 17 27.

Baumrind, D. 1967. "Childcare practices anteceding three patterns of preschool behavior," *Genetic Psych Monographs*, 75:43–88.

Bennett, L., S. Wolin, and D. Reiss. 1988. "Deliberate family process: A strategy for protecting children of alcoholics," *British J. of Addiction.* 26: 821–29.

Berkman, L. and L. Syme. 1979. "Social networks, host

resistance, and mortality: a nine-year follow-up study of Alameda County residents," *Am. J. of Epidemiology*, 109: 186–204.

Bigler, Rebecca. 2009. Quoted in "See Baby Discriminate" by Po Bronson and Ashley Merryman. www.newsweek. com/2009/09/04/see-baby-discriminate.html

Birdwhistell, Ray. 1970. *Kinesics and Change: Essays on Body Motion Communication*. Philadelphia: University of Pennsylvania Press.

Bowlby, John. 1958. "The nature of the child's tie to his mother," *Int J Psychoanal* 39 (5): 350–73.

Brooks, Robert and Sam Goldstein. 2002. *Raising Resilient Children: Fostering Strength, Hope and Optimism in Your Child.* NewYork: McGraw-Hill.

Buss, David M. 2005. *The Handbook of Evolutionary Psychology.* New York: Wiley and Sons.

Child Welfare Information Gateway, Children's Bureau. 2010. Strengthening Families and Communities: 2010 Resource Guide. U.S. Department of Health and Human Services. (Accessed January 2011) http://www.childwelfare.gov/pubs/res_guide_2010/

Colten, H. and B. Altevogt, eds. 2006. *Sleep Disorders and Sleep Deprivation: An Unmet Public Health Problem.* Washington D.C.: The National Academies Press.

Damasio, Antonio. 1999. *The Feeling of What Happens: Body and Emotion in the Making of Consciousness.* Fort Washington, PA: Harvest Book Company.

Darwin, Charles. 1872. *The Expression of the Emotions in Man and Animals.* Third Edition. Oxford University Press.

Di Pelligrino, G., et al. 1992. "Understanding motor events: a neurophysiological study," *Experimental Brain Research*, 91: 176–180.

Epstein, N., et al. 2003. "The McMaster Model: A view of healthy family functioning," in Walsh, Froma. 2003. *Normal Family Processes*. Third edition. New York: Guilford Press. 581–607.

Fiese, B. et al. 2002. "A review of 50 years of research on naturally occurring family routines and rituals: Cause for celebration?" *J. Fam. Psychol.* 16 (4): 381–90.

Frankl, Viktor. 2006. *Man's Search for Meaning*. New York: Beacon Press.

Frederickson, B., R. Mancuso, C. Branigan, and M. Tugade. 2000. "The undoing effect of positive emotions," *Motivation and Emotion*, 24: 237–58.

Frederickson, Barbara. 2001. "The role of positive emotions in positive psychology," *American Psychologist*, 56 (3): 218–26.

Frey, W. and M. Langseth. 1985. *Crying: The Mystery of Tears*. Minneapolis: Winston Press.

Gleason, K., L. Jensen-Campbell, and W. Ickes. 2009. "The role of empathic accuracy in adolescents' peer relations and adjustment," *Personality and Social Psychology Bulletin*, 35: 997–1011.

Goleman, Daniel. 1997. *Emotional Intelligence: Why It Can Matter More Than IQ*. New York: Bantam Dell.

Goleman, Daniel, 2006. *Social Intelligence: The New Science of Social Relationships*. New York: Bantam Books.

Gottman, John. 1993. *What Predicts Divorce? The Relationship Between Marital Processes and Marital Outcomes*. London: Psychology Press.

Gottman, J. and R.W. Levenson. 1992. "Marital processes

predictive of later dissolution: behavior, physiology and health," *Journal of Personal and Social Psychology*, 63: 221–233.

Gottman, John and Nan Silver. 1994. *Why Marriages Succeed Or Fail: And How You Can Make Yours Last.* New York: Simon and Shuster.
_____. 2000. *The Seven Principles for Making Marriage Work.* New York: Three Rivers Press.

Eriksson, Peter. 1998. "Neurogenesis in the Adult Hippocampus," *Nature Medicine*, 4, 1313–17.

Hightower, E., B. Riley, and M. Borba. 2002. *Our Family Meeting Book: Fun and Easy Ways to Manage Time, Build Communication, and Share Responsibility Week by Week.* Minneapolis: Free Spirit Publishing.

Iacoboni, M. 2008. *Mirroring People: The New Science of How We Connect with Others*, New York: Farrar, Straus & Giroux.

Jackson, Don and William Lederer. 1968. The Mirages of Marriage, New York: W.W. Norton.

Katz, Phyllis. 2009. Quoted in "See Baby Discriminate" by Po Bronson and Ashley Merryman. (Accessed 9.4.09) www.newsweek.com/2009/09/04/see-baby-discriminate.html

Kubansky, L.D., D. Sparrow, P. Vokanas, and I. Kowachi. 2001. "Is the glass half empty or half full? A prospective study of optimism and coronary heart disease in the normative aging study," Psychosomatic Medicine, 63: 910–16.

Laumann, E., J.H. Gagnon, R.T. Michael, and S. Michaels. 1994. *The Social Organization of Sexuality: Sexual Practices in the United States.* Chicago: University of Chicago Press.

Ledoux, Joseph. 1998. *The Emotional Brain: The Mysterious Underpinnings of Emotional Life.* New York: Simon and Schuster.

Lee, S. et al. 2007. "Physical education and physical activity: Results from the School Health Policies and Programs Study 2006," *J. of School Health*, 77: 435–63.

Lun, J., S. Kesebir, and S. Oishi. 2008. "On feeling understood and feeling well: The role of interdependence," *Journal of Research in Personality*, 42 (6): 1623–28.

Lutz, A, J. Brefczynski-Lewis, T. Johnstone, and R. Davidson. 2008. "Regulation of the Neural Circuitry of Emotion by Compassion Meditation: Effects of Meditative Expertise." *Public Library of Science One,* 3 (3): 1–10.

Maccoby, E. and J. Martin. 1983. "Socialization in the context of the family: Parent-child interaction." In P. Mussen and E. Hetherington, *Handbook of Child Psychology: Volume 4. Socialization, Personality and Social Development.* New York: Wiley.

Mehrabian, Albert. 1981. *Silent Messages: Implicit Communication of Emotions and Attitudes.* Belmont, CA: Wadworth.

Mittleman, Murray, et al. 1995. "Triggering of acute myocardial infarction onset by episodes of anger," *American Heart Association, Inc.*, 92: 1720–25.

Moody, James. 2001. "Race, School Integration, and Friendship," American J of Soc, 107(3): 679–716.

National Survey of Children's Health. 2010. *Family Meals.* (Accessed October 2010) <www.childtrendsdatabank. org/?q=node/197>

"National Survey of Sexual Health and Behavior." 2010. *J. of Sexual Medicine.* Vol. 7, pp 243–373.

Newberg, Andrew and Waldman, Mark. 2009. *How God Changes Your Brain.* New York: Ballantine Books.

Nielsen//Net Ratings. (Accessed February 2004) <en_

us.nielsen.com/content/dam/Nielsen/en_us/documents>

Page, Angie, et al. 2010. "Children's screen viewing is related to psychological difficulties irrespective of physical activity," (Accessed October 11, 2010). <pediatrics.aappublications.org/cgi/content/abstract/peds.2010-1154v1>

Paul, Jordan and Margaret Paul. 2002. *Do I Have to Give Up Me to be Loved by You,* Center City, MI: Hazelden.

Penn, Mark and E. Kinney Zalesne. 2007. *Microtrends: The Small Forces Behind Tomorrow's Big Changes.* New York: Twelve.

Pennebaker, J. and H. Traue. 1993. "Inhibition and psychosomatic processes," in Traue, H. and Pennebaker, J., Editors. *Emotion, Inhibition and Health.* Cambridge: Hogrefe and Huber Publishers, 146–63.

Pew Forum on Religion and Public Life. 2008. *U.S. Religious Landscape Survey* <http://religions.pewforum.org/affiliations>

Ratey, John 2008. *Spark: The Revolutionary New Science of Exercise and the Brain.* Boston: Little, Brown and Company.

Rideout, V., U. Foehr, and D. Roberts. 2010. "Generation M-squared: Media in the Lives of 8- to 18-year olds," Menlo Park: Kaiser Family Foundation.

Simmons, Rachel. 2002. *Odd Girl Out: The Hidden Culture of Aggression in Girls,* New York: Harcourt.

Shriver, Maria. 2009. *The Shriver Report: A Woman's Nation Changes Everything,* Washington D.C.: Free Press.

Smith, David, and Gary Gates. 2002. *Gay and Lesbian Families in the United States: Same-Sex Unmarried Partner Households.* Human Rights Campaign.

Taffel, Ron. 2009. *Childhood Unbound: Saving Our Kids' Best*

Selves: Confident Parenting in a World of Change. New York: Free Press.

Tannen, Deborah. 2007. *You Just Don't Understand: Women and Men in Conversation* New York: Harper-Collins.

Tooby, J. and L. Cosmides. 1990. "The past explains the present: Emotional adaptations and the structure of ancestral environments." *Ethology and Sociobiology, 11,* 375–424.

Walsh, Froma. 2003. *Normal Family Processes.* New York: Guilford Press.

Westley, W. A., and N. B. Epstein. 1969. *The Silent Majority.* San Francisco: Jossey-Bass.

Wilcox, W. B., ed. 2009. *The State of Our Unions, Marriage in America 2009: Money and Marriage.* Charlottesville: The National Marriage Project and the Institute for American Values.

Wingart, Pat, and Barbara Kantrowitz, "The Science Of A Good Marriage," *Newsweek,* Apr. 26, 1999.

INDEX

A

absolutes, avoiding, 3
acceptance, of differences, 99–112
active children, 103
active listening, 5
activity levels, 102
adaptability, 37–40, 42–43, 47–48, 102, 133
adolescents, 39, 46, 52, 55, 66–68, 73–74, 78, 92, 97–98, 107, 126, 154
adrenalin, 18, 20
advice giving, 142–143
age-appropriate consequences, 74–75
aggression, 108–109
Ahrons, Constance, 80
alliances, family, 146–149
ambivalent attachment, 95
amygdala, 16, 17, 18, 158
anger
    affect of, on health, 23
    avoiding feelings of, 27
    being aware of own, 13–14
    at children, 75–76
    expressing, 29–30, 42
    releasing on your own, 30–32
    repressed, 23
    self-help resources for, 177
angry words, 21
anxiety, 53
anxious attachment, 95
apologies, 121
approach/withdrawal, 102
arguments

being "right" in, 142
    making up after, 143
    timeouts during, 20
    unsolvable, 141–142
assumptions, checking, 8
attachment styles, 93–97
attachment theory, 84–85, 93–97
attention span, 102–103
auditory learners, 105–106
authoritarian parents, 60–61, 65–67
authoritative parents, 60–62
authority, 125–126
autonomy, 85, 89, 90–91
avoidant attachment, 95–96

B

Baumrind, Diana, 60
bedtime routines, 46–47, 52, 54
beliefs, 113–114
blame, 119, 120, 172
body language, 6
boundaries
    awareness of, 87–88
    healthy, 89–90, 149–150
    lack of, 88–89
Bowlby, John, 84
brain
    amygdala, 16, 17, 18, 158
    effect of romantic love on the, 150–151
    emotions and the, 16
brain cells, 47–48
brain research, vi, 123
brainstorming, 132
breathing, deep, 11
Brooks, Robert, 38

C

cell phones, 77–78
change
adapting to, 35–49
developmental, 38–40
in family structure, 36–37
initiating, 165–173
resilience to, 37–38
rites of passage, 40–41
roadblocks to, 169–171
self-help resources for adapting to, 178–179
social supports for dealing with, 44–45
unanticipated events and, 40
character education, 113
check-off lists, 54
childhood development, 38–40
childhood issues
dealing with past, 156–159
expressing feelings about, 27–28
as roadblock to being positive, 115
children
alone time with, 57
behavioral differences among, 22, 39
differences in temperaments of, 101–104
difficult, active, or feisty, 103, 170–171
diversity of, 37
easy/flexible, 103
impact of divorce on, 79–80, 152–153
increased responsibility and freedom for, 75
involving in family changes, 167
learning through imitating by, 33, 136
misbehaving by, 71–74
misinterpretation of nonverbal

messages by, 8–9
naming of, 51
need for autonomy by, 85
need for closeness by, 84–85
resilient, 38
respect for, 65
shy/cautious, 104
sleep deprivation in, 46–47
slow to warm up, 104
taking on roles of parent, 79
teaching by example, 67–68
wielding of power by, 63–64
yelling at, 75–76
closeness
balancing with distance, 84–98, 182
creating more, 92–93
desire for, 84–85
life cycle changes and shifts in need for, 97–98
too much, 88–89
cohabitation, 37
communication
characteristics of healthy, 2
context for, 9
elements of effective, 2–3
of feelings, 13–15
gender differences in, 108–109
importance of, 1–2, 12
killers, 139-141
listening, 3–5, 144
misunderstandings in, 6–7
nonverbal, 5–9
positive, 24
self-help resources for, 175–176
timing of, 9–10
tips and tools for, 9–12
compassion, 123
computers, 77–78
conflict, unresolved, 141–142
conflict avoiders, 137–138
conflict resolution, 10–11, 18, 120, 137–138

consequences
    age-appropriate, 74–75
    for negative behavior, 75–76
contempt, 139–140
co-parenting, 79–81
corporal punishment, 67, 81–82
cortisol, 20
couples. *See also* marriage;
  relationship(s)
    advice giving and, 142–143
    bonding between, 85–87
    characteristics of healthy,
        137–138
    conflict avoiders, 137–138
    cultivating intimacy and
        friendship in, 145–146
    making up by, 143
    unsolvable problems between,
        141–142
    validating, 137, 138
    volatile, 137
couples counseling, 141
criticism, 139, 140
crying
    comforting others when, 28–29
    ineffective, 26–27
    release through, 25–26
    relief from, 44–45
    with someone else, 28–29
cultural differences, 21–22, 105–
    107
cultural norms, 36
Current Family Assessment, vii,
    x–xiv

D

Dali Lama, 123
Damasio, Antonio, 23
Darwin, Charles, 15
decision-making
    barriers to good, 128–129
    inclusive, 125–126

stages of, 127–128
    tips for, 133–134
defense mechanisms, 28, 128
defensiveness, 139, 140
depression, 14, 23
developmental changes, 38–40
differences
    accepting, 99–112
    cultural and ethnic, 21–22,
        106–108
    gender, 108–109
    learning, 104–106
    religious, 111
    self-help resources for accepting,
        182–183
    in sexual orientation, 109–110
    in temperament, 101–104
difficult children, 103, 170–171
disagreements. *See* arguments
discipline, 60, 63, 64, 70–73, 82–
    83. *See also* limit setting
disorganized attachment, 96–97
distance
    balancing with closeness, 84–98,
        182
    life cycle changes and shifts in
        need for, 97–98
    too much, 91–93
distractibility, 103
diversity, 37. *See also* differences
divorce
    coping with, 42
    impact of, on children, 79–80,
        152–153
    predictors of, 139–141
    retaining rituals and routines
        after, 52
divorced families, parenting
    together in, 152–153
divorce rate, 37
dopamine, 150

E

easy/flexible children, 103
ego, 120
emotional bonding, 86
emotional disengagement, 140–141, 151
emotional flooding, 18–21
emotional intelligence, 22, 105
emotional mind, 16, 157
emotional reactions, 17–18
emotional self-awareness, 22
emotional self-regulation, 15
emotions. *See* feelings and emotions
empathy, 22, 33, 94, 123
ethnic diversity, 37, 106–108
excitement, 24
exercise, 47–48
expectations
    of children, 61, 70
    converting into preferences, 101
    cultural, 45
extended family, 51
eye contact, 6

F

facial expressions, 6, 15
families
    developmental changes in, 38–40
    extended, 51
    having fun as, 56–57
    importance of, 50
    nuclear, v, 36
    overly permissive, 63–65
    overly strict, 65–67
    rites of passage in, 40–41
    rituals and routines of, 51–59
    role models for, v–vi
    sharing time together by, 51–59
    in twenty-first century, 36–37
    value of, v

Family Alliance Exercise, 147
family alliances, 146–149
family cohesion, 86–93
family connections, 50–51
family goals, setting, 166–167
family mealtimes, 55–56
family meetings, 129–133, 167
Family of Origin Assessment, viii, 159–164
family roles, 117
family rules, 67–69
family structure, 35–37, 52, 60–61, 64, 83, 125, 146–147, 168
family systems theory, vi–vii
family time, 50–59
fear, 92–93
fear reactions, 17–18
feelings and emotions, 108–109
    being aware of own, 13–14
    as contagious, 33–34
    crying and, 25–27
    differences in expression of, 21–22
    expressing, 13–34, 42
    harnessing, 22
    holding in, 14
    identifying real, 20–21
    managing, 22, 34
    negative, 13–15, 22–23, 42, 75–76
    positive, 13, 22–23, 24, 114, 123
    primary, 15–16
    purpose of, 15
    repressed, 23
    self-help resources for expressing, 176–178
    sharing, 10–11
    triggers of, 157
    unexpressed, 115
fight-flight-freeze response, 17–18, 28
firmness, 60
Fisher, Helen, 150

flexible children, 103
forgiveness, 119–121
Four Horsemen, 139-140
Frankl, Viktor, 122
Frederickson, Barbara, 114
Frey, William, 44–45
friendship, 145–146

G

gender differences, 21–22, 108–109
gender roles, changes in, 36
gestures, 6
goal setting, 166–167
Golden Rule, 118–119
Goldstein, Sam, 38
Goleman, Daniel, 16, 22
Gottman, John, 18, 19, 137, 139–141
gratitude, 114
grief
   experiencing, 42–43
   repressed, 23
   social supports for, 44–45
guilt, of working mothers, 36
gut feelings, 8

H

happiness, 123
hardships, finding larger purpose in, 121–122
health
   affect of negative emotions on, 23
   benefits of exercise to, 47–48
heart disease, 23
holidays, 53
homosexuality, 109–110
household, changes in, 37
housework, sharing, 118

I

"I" messages, 3, 120, 129–130
imitation, learning through, 33, 136
immigration, 107
inborn traits, 22
independence, 97
indulgent parents, 61
infants, 52, 71, 84, 94–97, 102, 108
intelligence, 105
interaction patterns, 117–118
interfaith marriages, 111
Internet, 37, 76
interracial marriage, 106–107
intimacy, 93, 96, 97
   cultivating, 145–146
   desire for, 84–85

J

Jackson, Don, 145
joy, 114

K

kinesthetic learners, 106

L

learning, through imitation, 33, 136
learning differences, 104–106
Lederer, William, 145
LeDoux, Joseph, 16
letting go, 90
life cycle changes, 97–98
limbic system, 16
limit setting, 63, 70–71, 167–168
   changing methods of, 82–83
   in single parent families, 78–79, 154
   in stepfamilies, 79–81
   with technology, 76–78
listening. *See also* communication

active, 5
balancing with talking, 2
effective, 4–5
importance of, 3–4
to partner, 144
self-help resources for, 175–176
loss
coping with, 41–44
self-help resources for dealing
with, 178–179
social supports for dealing with,
44–45
love, 24, 60, 145, 150–151

M
marriage. *See also* couples;
relationship(s)
cultivating intimacy and
friendship in, 145–146
decline in rate of, 36–37
interfaith, 111
interracial, 106–107
keys to happy, 137–138
predictors of trouble in, 139–
141
sex in, 150–152
stages in, 98
unsolvable problems in, 141–
142
McMaster Model of Family
Functioning, 127–128
mealtimes, 55–56
meaning of life, 121–122
meditation, 123
memories, 157
men
crying by, 45
expression of emotions by,
108–109
stress reactions of, 19
minimal encouragers, 4
mirror neurons, 33, 45, 136

mistakes, 114, 116, 120
misunderstandings, 6–7
mixed messages, 7
moods
contagious nature of, 33–34,
117–118
differences in, 102
self-help resources for, 177–178
Moody, James, 107
moral education, 113–114
mourning, 42
mutual respect, 145

N
negative behaviors
age-appropriate consequences
for, 74–75
changing, 71–74
negative emotions
expressing, 13–15
reducing, 75–76
releasing, 42
value of, 22–23
neglectful parents, 60, 61
neurons, 47–48
neurotransmitters, 150
Nietzche, Friedrich, 122
nonverbal communication
importance of, 5–7
improving, 7–9
normal, defining, 36

O
open-ended questions, 4
optimism, 23, 114
over-involvement, 88–91
oxytocin, 150

P
parenting
challenges of, 19

in divorced families, 152–153
in single parent families, 154
parenting books, vi, 60, 175–187
parenting styles, 60–67
parents
adaptability of, to
developmental changes, 38–40
authoritarian, 60–61, 65–67
authoritative, 60–63
over-involved, 88–91
permissive/indulgent, 60, 61,
63–65
power of, 75
relationship between, 135–146
as role models, 70
single, 78–79
uninvolved/neglectful, 60, 61
working, v
working together as, 69–70,
135–155
passive-aggressive behavior, 14
past history, impact of, on present,
156–164
Paul, Jordan, 144
Paul, Margaret, 144
permissive parents, 60–65
persistence, 102–103
pessimism, 23
physical education, 47
physical punishment, 66, 81–82
playing, as family, 56–57
positive attitude, 113–124, 183–184
positive behaviors, reinforcing,
72–73
positive emotions, 13, 22–24, 114,
123
power
in relationships, 33–34
wielding of, by children, 63–64
praise, 72–74, 114, 115
primary emotions, 15–16
privacy, 89
problem behaviors

age-appropriate consequences
for, 74–75
changing, 71–74
problems, unresolved, 141–142
problem solving, 125–134, 185
professional help, 171–172
protectiveness, 66
psychosomatic symptoms, 14, 89
punishment
age-appropriate, 74–75
backfiring of, 115
harsh, 66–67
mild, 73–74
physical, 67, 81–82
purpose, sense of larger, 121–122

Q
questions, open-ended, 4

R
race relations, 106–108
racial diversity, 37
Ratey, John, 47
reality, respecting multiple views
of, 99–101, 142
reflexes, 17
reinforcements, positive, 72–73
relationship(s). *See also* couples;
marriage
advice giving and, 142–143
cultivating intimacy and
friendship in, 145–146
emotional disengagement in,
140–141, 151
between parents, 135–155
power in, 33–34
self-help resources for, 185–197
sibling, 158–159
supportive, 44–45
religion, 123
religious differences, 111
repair kit, for sharing feelings and

conflict resolution, 10–11
repressed emotions, 23
resentment, 116
resilience, 35, 37–38, 178
respect, 63, 68, 128, 145
responsibility, 75, 116–117, 121, 172
rhythmicity, 102
rites of passage, 40–41
rituals
    creating own, 57–58
    importance of, 51–53
role models, v–vi, 70
roles, 117
routines
    developing, 53–54
    importance of, 51–53
rules, 60, 67–69, 77, 117, 168

S
safety rules, 68
Satir, Virginia, 147
screen time, 76–78
secure attachment, 94
self-care, 45–46, 78, 116
self-esteem, 1–2, 14, 64, 72, 82
self-help resources, 171, 175–187
sensory threshold, 103
"The Serenity Prayer," 43–44
serotonin, 46
sex, 150–152
sexual orientation, 109–110
shy/cautious children, 104
sibling relationships, 158–159
single parent families
    limit setting in, 78–79
    parenting in, 154
sleep, 46–47
slow to warm up children, 104
social supports, 44–45
spanking, 67, 81–82
speaking for yourself, 2–3

spirituality, 31, 43 111, 113–114, 121, 195
star charts, 54
stepfamilies
    limit setting in, 79–81
    parenting in, 153
stonewalling, 139–140
stress, 16
    reactions to, 17–20
    resiliency and, 37–38
stress hormones, 18, 20
structure, 60
subjective truth, 142
systems theory, vi–vii

T
tactile learners, 106
Taffel, Ron, 76–77
talking. *See also* communication
    balancing with listening, 2
    making time for, 12
    self-help resources for, 175–176
    speaking for yourself, 2–3
Tannen, Deborah, 109
technological changes, 37, 75–76
teenagers, 39, 46, 52, 55, 66–68, 73–74, 78, 92, 97–98, 107, 126, 154
television, 77, 78
temperament, 22, 39, 101–104
texting, 78
therapeutic exercise, 30–32
therapy, when to seek, 171–172
time, spending together, 50–59, 179
timeouts, 20, 74
tone of voice, 6
transitions, 97–98
triggers, emotional, 157
tweens, 74

U

uninvolved parents, 60, 61

V
validators, 137, 138
vasopressin, 150
videogames, 78
viewpoints, respecting multiple,
  99–101, 142
volatile couples, 137

W
women
  expression of emotions by,
    108–109
  stress reactions of, 19
  in workforce, v
workforce, women in, v
working mothers, 36
working parents, v

Y
yelling, 75–76

ACKNOWLEDGMENTS

This book began twenty years ago as part of our effort to provide therapists in training with a clear understanding of families. Needless to say, the material has gone through thousands of permutations and augmentations through the years. For the past six months we have constantly been "just three weeks away" from completion.

This "project" (because it is so much more than a book) crystallized with the help and support of so many dear friends, family, and colleagues. We first give heartfelt thanks for the editorial assistance of Ilene Segalove, Bob Hartzell, and Kjell Rudestam. Each had an amazing ability to climb into our vision and help sort through a maze of possible presentation options. We also want to thank the many mentors in our lives who have paved the way, taught and encouraged us, including Virginia Satir, Salvador Minuchin, Charlie Fishman, Larry and Evelyn Thomas, Ron Taffel, Robert Brooks, Ram Dass, Brother David Steindl-Rast, Jordan Paul, and Maurice Elias.

We have deep love and appreciation for the whole staff of the Family Therapy Institute of Santa Barbara. Extraordinarily loyal and committed, several of our senior staff have given decades of invaluable support and fodder for our thinking. Our board of directors, equally loyal, has provided unwavering assistance throughout this time.

We give special thanks to each of our moms for continuing to grow, thrive, and be happy through loss and changes aplenty. We are grateful for your ideas, editorial inputs, and the encouragement to chase our dreams.

We also appreciate the many families and individuals we have treated but who have been such a "treat" to us in return. They have shared their hearts and souls and stories in a way that has helped us to refine our thinking and approaches at least a zillion times. They have shown us where we have gotten stuck, and taught us how to move on.

Finally, we would really like to acknowledge each other. We feel immensely proud and happy that we are alive and more in love each day. We have survived and thrived through the rigors of writing this book, which combined tons of work with countless, precious moments of teasing, prodding, supporting, and debating.

As for the tools that we have shared in these pages, the proof of the pudding is in our ability to co-create so many wonderful gifts throughout our marriage: the Institute that we direct, the two houses we built, and the fine young men that our sons have become. We want to thank Sean and Cree for being our very best teachers, and for finally getting over thinking that it was the worst thing in the world to have two "shrinks" for parents.

ABOUT THE AUTHORS

Don and Debra are a team both at home and at the office. Husband and wife for almost thirty years, they have simultaneously served as directors of the Family Therapy Institute of Santa Barbara, a nonprofit organization. In this capacity they oversee the clinical work of fourteen therapists providing help to hundreds of clients each year. They are authors or coauthors of numerous articles on parenting and clinical issues. In 2009, Don won the title of "Best Family Therapist" in a poll taken by SBParent.com. In 2010, Debra was honored with an Award for Service to the Community by local therapists and the mayor of Santa Barbara "for thirty years of inspiration, leadership, and training provided to thousands of clinicians, and the devotion exemplified in consistent visionary work for the community."

Don has a bachelor's degree from Dartmouth, a master's in school-child psychology from University of Virginia, and a Ph.D. in clinical psychology from California School of Professional Psychology. Also a musician, he was songwriter and music director for the animated PBS hit, *Jay Jay the Jet Plane.* His public education efforts have culminated in the writing and production of *Kids' EPs,* a series of songs

and activities that help young children with social and emotional learning. His music has won over ten major awards.

Debra received her undergraduate degree in psychology with distinction from Stanford University and her master's in social welfare from University of California at Berkeley with a specialty in family therapy and community mental health. Prior to founding the Institute in 1979, she was the executive director of Social Advocates for Youth in the San Francisco Bay Area, working with runaway teens and children at risk. She has taught marriage and family therapy at Antioch University, Pacifica Graduate Institute, numerous local agencies, schools, and mental health facilities. She finds respite from her busy life through painting, hiking, and being with her much loved dog, Shammy.

Don and Debra have lived in Santa Barbara, California, for over thirty years. They share a love of games, music, movies, biking, hiking, travel, and art.

Don and Debra are available for lectures, keynote presentations and workshops that range from a few hours to a few days, either as co-presenters or as individuals. They offer workshops to the general public, teachers and mental health professionals.

They have provided advanced training, consultation and supervision for over 30 years. They consult with non-profit counseling centers, medical, legal and law enforcement agencies, private businesses and individuals.

Areas of expertise include systems analysis, law and ethics, on-site case consultation, social and emotional learning, and training in specific topics regarding work with couples, families, teens and children.

Other Great Materials by Don MacMannis, Ph.D. (a.k.a. Dr. Mac)

Kids' EPs
by Dr. Mac & Friends

Award-winning PBS songwriter.

Fun and fabulous, adult-quality music with a message!

Winner:
iParenting Media Award

Teacher's Choice Award

Best Vacation Children's Product Award

National Parenting Center's Seal of Approval

Seal of Excellence Award, Creative Child Magazine

Kids' EPs Workbook: Hands-on Activities for Social, Emotional and Character Development
This 125-page activity book includes the kids' lyrics and coloring pages from all 8 of the KidsEPs albums plus adds more than a hundred lessons and activities for parents and teachers to share with kids.

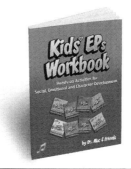

8 Great Themes:

Friends & Sharing
Social Skills & Bullying
Feelings & Fears
Practice & Success
Talking & Listening
Manners & Character
Happiness & Attitude
Respect & Responsibility

Listen to samples at
KidsEPs.com

25732429R00124

Made in the USA
Lexington, KY
01 September 2013